HOW TO BUILD WEALTH ON ANY INCOME

Think You Need a Huge Salary to Become Wealthy? Think Again

By Alex Carter

© 2025 Alex Carter

All rights reserved. No part of this publication may be reproduced, stored in a retrieval system, or transmitted in any form by any means, electronic, mechanical, photocopying, recording, or otherwise, without the prior written permission of the author.

This book is a work of nonfiction. While the stories shared are inspired by real experiences, some names and identifying details have been changed to protect privacy.

Published by Edenroot Press
edenrootpress.com

Contents

About the Author 15

Acknowledgements 16

Introduction: Wealth Isn't Reserved for High Earners 18

    The Big Lie: You Need a High Salary to Build Wealth 19

    The Hidden Advantage of Starting Small 20

    What You'll Learn in This Book 20

    The Real Definition of Wealth 22

    Wealth Is a Mindset and a System, Not an Income Bracket 22

    Why This Book Matters Right Now 23

    Let's Begin, From Exactly Where You Are 24

Chapter 1: Redefining Wealth Beyond Salary 26

    What Is Real Wealth, Anyway? 26

    High Income ≠ Financial Freedom 27

    Stop Focusing on Paycheques, Start Focusing on Assets 29

    Key Insight: It's Not How Much You Earn, It's What You Keep and Grow 30

    Real Story: Sarah the £25K Wealth Builder 31

    Why This Matters for You 32

    Your Wealth-Building Action for This Chapter.33

Takeaway: You're Already Wealthier Than You Think 34

Chapter 2: The Mindset of Everyday Millionaires 36

Millionaires Next Door: What the Research Reveals 36

Busting the Myths: No Luck, No Lottery, No Inheritance 37

The Millionaire Mindset: Habits Over Hustle 38

Consistency: The Real Millionaire Superpower 40

Real Story: Karen the Quiet Millionaire 41

Key Insight: Millionaire Status Is a Behaviour, Not a Pay Bracket 42

Your Wealth-Building Action for This Chapter . 43

Takeaway: The Quiet Millionaire Could Be You 44

Chapter 3: Tracking Every Pound with Purpose . 45

Budgeting Isn't Restriction, It's Empowerment 46

Intentional Spending: Every Pound Has a Job . 47

Create a Simple Money Tracking System 47

Clarity Beats Willpower Every Time 49

Real Story: Amelia Finds £500/Month by Plugging the Leaks 50

Your Wealth-Building Action for This Chapter . 52

    Takeaway: Tracking Is the First Step to Transformation 53

Chapter 4: Paying Yourself First, No Matter How Small 55

    Why Saving First Matters More Than How Much 56

    Automate to Eliminate Excuses 57

    Start Small, Build Momentum 58

    Real Story: From £20 to £500/Month, Callum's Journey 59

    Why This Works on Any Income 60

    Your Wealth-Building Action for This Chapter . 61

    Takeaway: You Are Your First and Most Important Bill 62

Chapter 5: Slashing Lifestyle Inflation 64

    Why Most Raises Disappear Overnight 65

    Avoiding "Upgrade Syndrome" 66

    How to Keep Expenses Steady While Income Rises 67

    Key Insight: Living Below Your Means Is the Wealth Superpower 68

    Real Story: Emma and James, Student Budget, Wealthy Future 69

    Your Wealth-Building Action for This Chapter . 70

Takeaway: The Richest People Don't Look Rich 72

Chapter 6: Building an Emergency Fund on Any Income 73

    Why Emergency Savings Matter More Than You Think...73

    How to Save, Even on a Tight Budget...............75

    Creative Ways to Jumpstart Your Fund...........76

    Key Insight: Security First, Growth Second.....77

    Real Story: Maya's £1,000 Emergency Fund on Minimum Wage..78

    Your Wealth-Building Action for This Chapter.79

    Takeaway: Peace of Mind Is Priceless.............80

Chapter 7: Killing Consumer Debt Fast...............82

    Why Debt Sabotages Wealth Growth...............83

    The Two Fastest Ways to Pay Off Debt: Snowball vs Avalanche.....................................84

    How to Stay Motivated While Paying Off Debt.86

    Real Story: Jordan Pays Off £15,000 on a Modest Income..87

    Key Insight: Every Pound of Debt Paid Is a Pound Freed to Build Wealth............................88

    Your Wealth-Building Action for This Chapter.89

    Takeaway: Kill Debt, Reclaim Your Future.......90

Chapter 8: Automating Wealth-Building Habits...92

Why Automation Is Your Financial Superpower 93

The "Set It and Forget It" Approach to Wealth . 94

1. Automate Your Savings 94

2. Automate Your Investments 95

3. Automate Your Debt Payments 96

How Automation Removes Temptation and Friction 96

Real Story: Rachel's Wealth Built on Autopilot 97

Key Insight: Automation Builds Wealth When Motivation Fades 99

Your Wealth-Building Action for This Chapter 100

Takeaway: Systems Build Success, Not Willpower 101

Chapter 9: Growing Income Strategically 102

Why Cutting Expenses Alone Isn't Enough 103

How to Increase Your Income on the Side 103

Leveraging Existing Skills for Higher Earnings 106

Key Insight: You Don't Need a Second Job, You Need a Smarter Income Plan 107

Real Story: Amy's £500/Month Tutoring Side Hustle 107

Your Wealth-Building Action for This Chapter 108

Takeaway: Your Skills Are Seeds, Plant Them Wisely 110

Chapter 10: Avoiding the Big Money Traps 111

The Hidden Ways Small Incomes Stay Stuck . 112

Saying No to "Keeping Up Appearances" 114

Practising Conscious Consumption 115

Key Insight: Avoiding Mistakes Builds Wealth Just as Fast as Making Money 117

Real Story: Tariq's Turnaround Through Saying No 117

Your Wealth-Building Action for This Chapter 119

Takeaway: What You Don't Spend Is as Powerful as What You Earn 120

Chapter 11: Making Small Investments Early 122

Why Time Beats Amount in Investing 122

How to Start Investing with £10–£50 a Month 124

1. Choose a Platform 124

2. Open the Right Account 124

3. Pick a Simple Investment: Index Funds 125

4. Automate and Forget 126

Key Insight: Every Pound Invested Buys Future Freedom 126

    Real Story: Priya's £50/Month to a Comfortable Future 127

    Your Wealth-Building Action for This Chapter 129

    Takeaway: The Best Time to Invest Was Yesterday. The Second-Best Is Today. 130

Chapter 12: Buying Assets, Not Liabilities 132

    Assets vs Liabilities: The Defining Wealth Question 133

    Choosing Investments Over Consumption 134

    The Mindset Shift: From Spender to Asset-Builder 135

    Real Story: Darren Chooses Property Over Prestige 137

    Key Insight: Prioritise Things That Put Money in Your Pocket 138

    Your Wealth-Building Action for This Chapter 139

    Takeaway: Flashy Spenders Impress Today, Asset Builders Win Tomorrow 140

Chapter 13: Using Windfalls Wisely 142

    What Counts as a Windfall? 143

    Why Most People Blow It (and How to Avoid It) 144

    The Golden Rule of Windfalls: Split, Don't Spend 144

✅ The 50–30–20 Rule for Windfalls 145

3 Common Windfalls, And What to Do With Them 146

Key Insight: Windfalls Accelerate Wealth When Handled Intentionally 147

Real Story: Laura's £1,000 Bonus That Changed Everything 148

Your Wealth-Building Action for This Chapter 149

Takeaway: Windfalls Won't Build Wealth, *You* Will 150

Chapter 14: Teaching Wealth Principles to Family 152

Breaking Generational Money Patterns 153

Simple Ways to Raise Financially Savvy Kids (or Influence Family) 154

How to Influence Family Without Preaching .. 157

Key Insight: Teaching Multiplies Wealth Across Generations 159

Real Story: Malcolm Raises a Money-Smart Teen 160

Your Wealth-Building Action for This Chapter 161

Takeaway: You're Not Just Building Wealth, You're Building Legacy 162

Chapter 15: Building Wealth with Community Support 164

The Myth of the Lone Wealth Builder 164

Why Accountability Increases Success 165

How to Find a Wealth-Building Community 166

Avoiding Environments That Normalise Overspending 169

Real Story: Imran Finds Strength in Community 170

Key Insight: Community Keeps You Going When Motivation Dips 172

Your Wealth-Building Action for This Chapter 172

Takeaway: Wealth-Building Is Personal, But It Doesn't Have to Be Lonely 174

Chapter 16: Protecting Your Progress 175

Why Protection Is the Missing Piece in Wealth Conversations 176

The Most Common Threats to Wealth 177

The Three Layers of Financial Protection 178

Proactive Steps That Prevent Wealth Erosion 181

Real Story: Priya's Protection Plan Saved Her 183

Key Insight: Building Wealth Is Pointless If It's Vulnerable to Disaster 184

Your Wealth-Building Action for This Chapter 185

Takeaway: True Wealth Isn't Just What You Accumulate, It's What You Can Protect 186

Chapter 17: Multiplying Wealth Over Time 187

The Myth of "Getting Rich Quick" 188

Adding Income Streams as Confidence Grows 188

Scaling Savings and Investments as Income Increases 190

Staying Humble as Wealth Builds 192

Key Insight: Slow, Steady Scaling Wins 193

Real Story: Martina's 10-Year Journey to £100k 194

Your Wealth-Building Action for This Chapter 195

Takeaway: Wealth Grows When You Do, Gradually, Intentionally, Quietly 197

Chapter 18: Avoiding Sabotage as Income Grows 198

The Income Illusion: "I Make More, So I'm Fine" 198

The Sneaky Cost of Lifestyle Creep 199

Why Wealth Builders Stay Humble with More Income 201

12

How to Reaffirm Goals and Systems at Every Level 202

Real Story: Olivia's Wake-Up Call 204

Key Insight: Bigger Income = Bigger Responsibility 205

Your Wealth-Building Action for This Chapter 206

Takeaway: The Goal Isn't Just to Earn More, It's to Handle More with Wisdom 207

Chapter 19: Redefining Wealth as Freedom 209

Why True Wealth Isn't About Status or Things 210

Linking Financial Goals to Time Freedom, Peace, and Purpose 211

Avoiding the Trap of Endlessly Chasing "More" 212

Key Insight: Wealth Is Measured in Choices, Not Numbers 213

Real Story: Lewis Chose Freedom Over Status 214

Your Wealth-Building Action for This Chapter 215

Takeaway: Wealth Isn't the Destination, It's the Doorway 217

Chapter 20: Becoming a Wealth Builder for Life 218

Why Wealth-Building Is a Practice, Not a Goal 218

Staying Curious, Flexible, and Adaptive.........220

You Don't Need a Big Income, You Need Big Commitment 221

Every Pound Matters: Save It. Invest It. Protect It. 222

Real Story: Yasmin, the Quiet Millionaire 223

Your Wealth-Building Action for Life 224

Takeaway: You Are a Wealth Builder Now 226

Conclusion: You Already Have Enough to Start 227

Don't Wait for More, Use What You've Got.....228

Take One Small Wealth-Building Step Today.229

You Are Not Behind. You Are Beginning. 230

Final Words: You Don't Have to Earn More, You Just Have to Act Differently 231

About the Author

Alex Carter is an internationally recognised wealth mindset coach, financial empowerment speaker, and New York Times bestselling author. With over 20 years of experience in personal finance, entrepreneurship, and personal development, Alex has helped thousands transform their financial futures, not by chasing money, but by mastering their mindset.

From humble beginnings to building multiple streams of income and achieving financial independence, Alex's mission is clear: to help ordinary people create extraordinary financial lives, one powerful decision at a time.

When not writing, Alex can be found hiking with their dog, mentoring young entrepreneurs, or running money mindset workshops in under-resourced communities.

Acknowledgements

This book was written for the quiet achievers, the ones who never made headlines but consistently showed up, made smart choices, and proved that wealth has nothing to do with status and everything to do with mindset and action.

To every reader who picked up this book with a desire to change their financial future, thank you. You are the reason I do this work. Your commitment to building wealth from where you are inspires more than you know.

To the everyday wealth builders whose stories are woven throughout these pages, thank you for your courage and authenticity. Your experiences remind us that financial transformation is possible at any income level.

To my family and friends, thank you for your unwavering support, patience, and encouragement as I poured my energy into writing this series. You've kept me grounded while helping me dream bigger.

To the financial educators, authors, and researchers who've paved the way, your work continues to light the path. In particular, I'm grateful for insights from *The Millionaire Next Door*, the FIRE (Financial Independence, Retire Early) community, and countless personal finance thought leaders whose ideas have shaped this book.

And finally, to anyone who has ever felt like wealth was out of reach, this book is proof that it's not. The steps may be small, but when taken consistently, they will change your life.

Keep building. Keep learning. Keep believing.

With gratitude,
Alex Carter

Introduction: Wealth Isn't Reserved for High Earners

When Marcus landed his first full-time job at age 22, he was earning just £21,000 a year as a support worker in Birmingham. Most of his mates rolled their eyes when he talked about his budget or tried to avoid expensive nights out. "Mate, chill, it's not like you're going to get rich on that salary anyway," one friend said with a smirk.

But Marcus had other plans.

He started tracking every pound. He set aside just £25 a month in a stocks and shares ISA. He bought a bike to cut transport costs. He taught himself about index funds on YouTube after work. While others waited for a bigger paycheck to "get serious about money," Marcus got serious anyway.

Ten years later, at 32, Marcus still isn't a high earner, he now makes £36,000 a year in a management role, but he has over £110,000 in net worth. No inheritance. No lucky break. Just consistency, discipline, and a willingness to build wealth from where he was.

This book is for the Marcuses of the world. And for everyone who's ever thought, *"I'll start building wealth when I earn more."*

It's time to flip that belief on its head.

The Big Lie: You Need a High Salary to Build Wealth

We live in a culture obsessed with income.

Headlines scream about six-figure careers. Influencers parade their earnings online. Even conversations with friends and family often boil down to one question: *"How much do you make?"*

But here's the hard truth most people miss:
A high income does not guarantee wealth. And a modest income does not prevent it.

You can earn £120,000 a year and still live paycheque to paycheque. You can earn £25,000 and build a six-figure net worth over time. It's not how much you make, it's what you do with it.

In fact, many so-called "broke millionaires" are stuck on a financial treadmill: flashy salaries, flashy cars, flashy debt. Meanwhile, countless quiet, everyday earners are quietly building real financial security behind the scenes.

And the reason? **Wealth isn't built through income alone. It's built through systems, mindset, and daily decisions.**

The Hidden Advantage of Starting Small

You might think building wealth with a modest income is like trying to climb Everest in flip-flops. But here's the twist: starting with less can be one of your greatest advantages.

Why?

Because when you don't have money to waste, you learn to spend with intention.
 Because when your margin is tight, you're forced to prioritise what really matters.
 Because when you succeed on a small income, you develop unshakeable habits that will serve you for life, no matter how much you eventually earn.

This book isn't about limitation. It's about liberation.

You don't need to wait for a raise, a windfall, or a "better" job to start building wealth. You can start now. Right where you are. With exactly what you've got.

What You'll Learn in This Book

How to Build Wealth on Any Income is not a get-rich-quick book. It's a **get-rich-slow-but-sure** book.

It's about learning to think differently about money, and to act differently with money. You'll learn:

How to define wealth based on *net worth*, not income.

How everyday people, teachers, admin assistants, delivery drivers, quietly become millionaires.

How to master budgeting, saving, and investing even when every pound counts.

How to avoid the traps that keep small earners stuck, like lifestyle inflation, debt cycles, and emotional spending.

How to grow your income strategically, not just work more hours.

How to use discipline, automation, creativity, and consistency to your advantage.

And most importantly, how to believe that you are *already capable* of building wealth, without waiting for the "perfect" financial situation.

Each chapter will give you a practical principle, step-by-step tools you can use right away, and a real-life story of someone just like you, someone who started with little but built a lot.

The Real Definition of Wealth

Before we go any further, let's redefine what we're aiming for.

Wealth isn't about private jets or multi-million-pound mansions.
Wealth is about **freedom**.
Freedom from stress.
Freedom from living paycheque to paycheque.
Freedom to choose where you live, what you do, and how you spend your time.
Freedom to help others. To rest. To pursue what matters.

That kind of wealth?
That's available to *anyone* who's willing to take consistent, intentional action over time.

Including you.

Wealth Is a Mindset and a System, Not an Income Bracket

There's a reason people who win the lottery often go bankrupt within a few years. It's because wealth isn't about a lump sum, it's about a way of thinking and behaving.

It's knowing how to manage money, not just earn it.

It's choosing delayed gratification over short-term pleasure.

It's setting up automatic savings, rather than relying on willpower.

It's understanding the magic of compound interest, even with £10 a month.

Wealthy people aren't necessarily better or smarter. But they *think* differently. They make money decisions based on future value, not present mood. And that mindset? It's available to you.

You don't need a finance degree or a six-figure salary to become wealthy. You need a shift in how you see yourself and your money.

This book will give you that shift, along with the systems to back it up.

Why This Book Matters Right Now

We're living through financially uncertain times.

Prices are rising. Wages feel like they're standing still. And for many people, the dream of building wealth feels more out of reach than ever.

But here's what I believe, and what I've seen again and again:

You don't need certainty to build wealth. You need courage, commitment, and clarity.

This book will help you:

> Take control of your money, even when it feels like there's not much to control.
>
> Stop comparing yourself to others, and start building something real, meaningful, and lasting.
>
> Silence the voice that says, *"I'll never get ahead,"* and replace it with a new one that says, *"I've got this."*

Let's Begin, From Exactly Where You Are

No matter your income, your background, your past money mistakes, or your current financial stress, you are welcome here. You're not behind. You're not broken. You're not "too late."

You're just in the perfect place to start.

And starting is the most powerful wealth-building decision you can make.

Let's prove, together, that you don't need a six-figure salary to build a six-figure life.

Let's show the world what's possible when everyday people take control of their financial futures.

Because wealth isn't reserved for high earners.
It's built by anyone who's ready to take it seriously.

And I believe that person… is you.

Chapter 1: Redefining Wealth Beyond Salary

When people talk about success, they often start with one question: *"How much do you make?"*

It's a loaded question, and it's based on a faulty assumption.

We're conditioned to equate income with success, to see a higher salary as a sign of wealth. But here's the truth that will change your financial future forever:

Your salary is not your wealth. Your *net worth* is.

And the two couldn't be more different.

What Is Real Wealth, Anyway?

Let's break it down in simple terms.

> **Income** is the money you earn, your monthly paycheque, bonuses, freelance gigs, side hustles.
>
> **Wealth** is what you *keep*, the total value of your assets (savings, investments, property) minus your debts (credit cards, loans, overdrafts).

In other words, wealth is your *net worth*. It's the money that stays with you, grows over time, and gives you security and options.

You can have a high income and still have zero wealth. You can have a modest income and quietly build a solid financial foundation.

This distinction is everything.

Because until you stop chasing paycheques and start building *value*, you'll always feel like you're running uphill.

High Income ≠ Financial Freedom

It sounds counterintuitive, but it's shockingly common: people earning six figures who are drowning in stress, buried in debt, and living paycheque to paycheque.

They drive nice cars, live in posh neighbourhoods, wear designer clothes… and have no actual wealth to show for it.

Here's why:

> They spend in line with their income, or above it.

They rely on credit for lifestyle inflation.

They don't save or invest consistently.

They confuse status with security.

Take Jason, for example. He's a marketing director earning £110,000 a year. On paper, he's doing well. But his monthly outgoings, mortgage, lease payments, school fees, luxury holidays, and endless subscriptions, eat up every pound.

At 42, he has less than £5,000 in savings and £18,000 in credit card debt. He feels trapped, exhausted, and unsure where his money actually goes.

Then there's Emma. She works as a primary school teaching assistant, earning £25,000 a year. She budgets meticulously, saves 20% of her salary, avoids debt, and invests monthly in low-cost index funds.

At 42, Emma has a net worth of over £100,000 and is on track to retire comfortably.

Same age. Very different incomes. Totally different financial outcomes.

The difference? **One is building a lifestyle. The other is building wealth.**

Stop Focusing on Paycheques, Start Focusing on Assets

To shift from an income mindset to a wealth mindset, you must focus on three key areas:

Assets: These are things that grow your net worth. Savings accounts, ISAs, investment portfolios, property, pension funds, even skills that help you earn more over time.

Savings: Wealth builders don't just earn, they keep. That means prioritising saving even when it feels small. A tenner saved is worth more than a raise that gets instantly spent.

Investments: Putting money into things that generate income or grow in value over time is how you multiply your wealth. This could be stocks, index funds, or eventually, property or business ventures.

The goal isn't just to bring money in, it's to **keep it**, **grow it**, and let it work for you.

Because unlike your salary, which stops when you do… your assets don't sleep.

Key Insight: It's Not How Much You Earn, It's What You Keep and Grow

Let's get practical.

Imagine two people:

> **Dan** earns £90,000/year but spends £92,000/year and carries £15,000 in debt.

> **Priya** earns £25,000/year, lives below her means, saves £250/month, and avoids consumer debt.

After one year:

> Dan's net worth has gone *down*.

> Priya's has gone *up* by £3,000, plus any interest or investment returns.

Now imagine this over ten years. Dan's stuck in a hamster wheel. Priya has £30,000+ saved or invested, not including growth. She has freedom, security, and choices.

Dan's not the exception, he's the rule. So is Priya.

Wealth doesn't come from what you make, it comes from what you do *consistently* with what you make.

Real Story: Sarah the £25K Wealth Builder

Sarah works full-time as a receptionist at a GP surgery in Nottingham. She earns just under £25,000 a year. For most people around her, money is always tight, and there's a sense that "it is what it is."

But Sarah approached things differently from day one.

In her early twenties, she started tracking every expense. She ditched takeaways, paused her Netflix subscription, and shopped second-hand. She built up an emergency fund of £1,000 within her first year, just £20 at a time.

Next, she opened a Lifetime ISA and began putting away £100/month, boosted by the 25% government bonus.

Then she discovered index funds through a podcast and started investing £150/month through a stocks and shares ISA. She also picked up weekend dog walking gigs to boost her income by £200/month.

By age 35, Sarah had no debt, £18,000 in cash savings, and over £85,000 in investment accounts.

Her total net worth? Just over **£100,000**.

All while never earning more than £26,000 in a single year.

How?

> She didn't wait for a raise, she started with what she had.
>
> She avoided lifestyle inflation.
>
> She tracked her money and gave every pound a job.
>
> She stuck to the basics, stayed consistent, and trusted the process.

Sarah's not flashy. But she's wealthy.

Why This Matters for You

You don't need a degree in finance or a fancy job title to build wealth.

You need to:

> Know what real wealth is (net worth, not salary).
>
> Shift focus from spending to saving and investing.

Take consistent action, even if it feels small.

Trust that small steps, repeated over time, become something massive.

And here's the best part: because you're starting from a realistic place, every pound you save, invest, or protect carries even more power. You'll build the muscle of discipline early, and that will serve you long after your income eventually increases.

Your Wealth-Building Action for This Chapter

Let's get tactical. Here's how to apply what you've just learned:

Calculate Your Net Worth

- Add up all your assets (cash, savings, investments, etc.).

- Subtract all your debts (credit cards, loans, overdrafts).

- The result is your starting point, not your endpoint.

Start Thinking in Net Worth Terms

Ask yourself regularly: *"Will this decision grow or shrink my net worth?"*

Track, Don't Judge

This isn't about guilt or shame. It's about awareness. You can't grow what you don't track.

Commit to Saving or Investing Something This Month

Even if it's £10. It's the *habit* that matters, not the amount.

Takeaway: You're Already Wealthier Than You Think

If you've been measuring your success solely by your income, it's time to stop.

You are not your paycheque.
You are not your job title.
And you are not stuck.

You are a potential wealth builder, right now, right here, with exactly what you've got.

And when you start thinking in terms of *net worth*, you'll begin to see money not as something that comes and goes, but as something you can build, protect, and grow.

Welcome to the mindset shift that changes everything.

Chapter 2: The Mindset of Everyday Millionaires

When you think of a millionaire, who comes to mind?

Maybe someone cruising through Mayfair in a Bentley. Maybe a tech entrepreneur sipping cocktails in Dubai. Or maybe a flashy influencer who "made it" overnight.

But let me introduce you to someone very different.

Meet Geoff.

Geoff is a 54-year-old electrician from Hull. He's worked for the same family-run company for nearly 30 years. He wears worn-out boots, packs his own lunch, and drives a sensible second-hand van. You wouldn't look twice at him on the street.

Geoff's annual salary? Around £36,000.

But Geoff's net worth? Just over **£1.1 million**.

No lottery. No inheritance. No fancy side hustle. Just habits, consistency, and the mindset of an everyday millionaire.

Millionaires Next Door: What the Research Reveals

In their landmark book *The Millionaire Next Door*, researchers Thomas J. Stanley and William D. Danko studied hundreds of self-made millionaires in the UK and the US. What they found turned conventional wisdom on its head.

Most millionaires weren't high-flying executives or celebrities.
They didn't live in mansions or drive sports cars.
In fact, many of them lived in modest homes, drove used cars, and made average incomes.

So how did they become wealthy?

Through **behavioural patterns** and **mindset principles**, not massive paycheques.

They were frugal.
They were consistent savers.
They invested early and regularly.
They avoided debt.
They valued independence over status.
They lived well *below* their means for decades.

In short: millionaire status was something they *practised*, not something they *earned*.

Busting the Myths: No Luck, No Lottery, No Inheritance

There are three persistent myths about millionaires that keep everyday people stuck. Let's bust them right now:

Myth 1: Most millionaires inherited their money

False. According to multiple studies, **8 out of 10 millionaires are self-made**. That means they built their wealth from the ground up, no trust fund, no silver spoon.

Myth 2: You have to get lucky

Sure, some people stumble into wealth. But most everyday millionaires didn't win anything, they *planned*, *worked*, and *waited*. They played the long game while others looked for shortcuts.

Myth 3: You need a high-paying job

Not true. Many millionaires come from jobs like teachers, mechanics, postal workers, or admin staff. What sets them apart isn't their salary, it's their decisions.

So if you've ever thought, *"That could never be me,"* it's time to reconsider.

The Millionaire Mindset: Habits Over Hustle

Let's break down some of the key mindsets and habits shared by self-made millionaires.

1. They Think in Decades, Not Days

Wealthy people know that *time* is their greatest asset. They don't expect overnight results, they expect gradual, consistent growth. They embrace the power of compound interest, long-term investing, and patience.

> "I'm not trying to look rich this year. I'm trying to be rich in 10 years."

2. They Live Below Their Means

Millionaires focus on *margin*, the gap between what they earn and what they spend. They avoid lifestyle creep. They keep expenses low even when income rises. They don't "upgrade" just because they can.

3. They Avoid Bad Debt Like the Plague

You won't find a garage full of financed toys in the millionaire mindset. They pay cash, avoid credit card balances, and refuse to borrow for depreciating assets. Debt slows down wealth, it's that simple.

4. They Prioritise Saving and Investing

Millionaires pay themselves first. They automate savings. They invest regularly in stocks, pensions, property, or business ventures. They don't wait for "extra money", they build wealth by making it a non-negotiable.

5. They Don't Chase Approval

They're not obsessed with looking successful. In fact, many millionaires intentionally avoid flashy lifestyles because they care more about freedom than image.

They don't care if their neighbours know they're wealthy. They care if they can sleep at night knowing they're financially secure.

Consistency: The Real Millionaire Superpower

Here's a secret: most people *could* become millionaires. The reason they don't? Inconsistency.

They start budgeting, then stop.
They invest for a bit, then pull out.
They save for three months, then splurge on a holiday.

Millionaires aren't perfect. But they are *persistent*. They do the boring stuff over and over again. They keep going when it's slow. They stay committed when no one's watching.

That's the magic. Not a big salary. Not a side hustle explosion. Just **small, consistent behaviours** that snowball over time.

Real Story: Karen the Quiet Millionaire

Karen works as a nurse in Manchester. She started on £22,000 a year in her early twenties. Over the years, her salary grew modestly, but she never earned more than £38,000.

She never looked rich. She shopped at charity shops, brought her lunch to work, and kept the same car for 15 years.

But here's what Karen did:

> She saved at least 15% of every paycheque.

> She maxed out her workplace pension contributions.

> She invested in a stocks and shares ISA monthly, starting with just £50.

> She lived in a modest home she bought at 28 and never moved "up."

> She tracked her spending every month.

By 52, Karen's mortgage was paid off. Her ISA and pension were worth over £700,000. Add in cash savings and other assets, and Karen's net worth quietly crossed the million-pound mark.

She didn't go viral. She didn't launch a business. She didn't inherit a fortune.

She just did the simple things, consistently.

Key Insight: Millionaire Status Is a Behaviour, Not a Pay Bracket

Let that sink in: **becoming a millionaire is more about behaviour than salary.**

If you:

>   Save consistently,

>   Spend intentionally,

>   Invest early and often,

>   Avoid unnecessary debt, and

>   Think long-term…

…you are practising the exact same habits that build real wealth.

You're already acting like a millionaire, even if your bank balance doesn't show it yet.

And eventually? It will.

Your Wealth-Building Action for This Chapter

Let's apply what you've learned.

Write Your Millionaire Habits List

Choose 3 behaviours you can start or improve this month (e.g., automate savings, review subscriptions, start investing £25/month).

Identify and Bust Your Own Millionaire Myths

Be honest: do you believe you *need* a big salary to build wealth? Why? Challenge that belief in writing.

Commit to Long-Term Thinking

Write a note to your future self 10 years from now. What do you want your net worth, habits, and financial freedom to look like?

These exercises might seem simple. But they're building the mindset muscle you'll use to create real wealth.

Takeaway: The Quiet Millionaire Could Be You

You don't have to earn six figures to live a six-figure life.
You don't have to win the lottery to win with money.
And you definitely don't need anyone's permission to start thinking like a millionaire, starting today.

Because it's not flashy choices that build wealth. It's quiet ones.
It's not sudden windfalls, it's slow growth.
And it's not about income, it's about behaviour.

So start behaving like a millionaire.
Because the mindset always comes before the money.

Chapter 3: Tracking Every Pound with Purpose

When Amelia first sat down to look at her monthly expenses, she expected to find a few surprises, maybe an unused subscription or two. What she didn't expect was this:

Over **£500 a month** disappearing into things she barely noticed.

Daily takeaways. Forgotten free trials. Petrol station snacks. Impulse Amazon buys. All harmless on their own, until she saw the total.

That day changed everything.

She didn't get a new job. She didn't get a raise. But she *did* get serious about tracking her money.

Six months later, she'd paid off two credit cards and built her first emergency fund. Same income. New results.

All because she learned the most underrated secret in personal finance:

If you don't track it, you can't improve it.

Budgeting Isn't Restriction, It's Empowerment

The word "budget" often makes people wince.

It feels like a diet for your bank account. No fun. No freedom. Just guilt, spreadsheets, and stress.

But here's the truth: **a budget isn't a cage. It's a compass.**

A budget doesn't tell you what you *can't* do, it shows you what you *can*. It replaces stress with clarity. Regret with control.

When you track your money, you're not just keeping records. You're reclaiming power.

Think about it:

> You wouldn't drive across the country without a map.

> You wouldn't build a house without a blueprint.

> So why live your financial life without a plan?

Budgeting gives you *choice*. And choice is freedom.

Intentional Spending: Every Pound Has a Job

One of the biggest mindset shifts in building wealth is this: stop spending *mindlessly*, and start spending *intentionally*.

Intentional spending means:

> You *know* where your money is going.

> You *choose* where it goes in advance.

> You *align* your spending with your values, goals, and priorities.

That's a far cry from the default mode most people live in, where money drips out of their accounts in a thousand tiny leaks they don't even notice.

Here's a question to ask yourself this week:

> "If I looked at my last 30 days of spending, would I be proud of how I used my money?"

If the answer is no, don't beat yourself up. But do get curious. Because that's where change begins.

Create a Simple Money Tracking System

You don't need to become a financial analyst to take control of your money.

All you need is a simple system. Here's a 3-step process that works, even for people who hate budgeting.

Step 1: Know What's Coming In

List every source of income, salary, benefits, side gigs, anything.

✓ *Tip:* Use your net (after-tax) income to avoid overestimating.

Step 2: Know What's Going Out

Break your spending into three categories:

Fixed Expenses – Rent, bills, subscriptions

Variable Essentials – Groceries, transport, petrol

Discretionary Spending – Takeaways, entertainment, online shopping

Track every pound for one month, even the coffee.

✓ *Tip:* Use a budgeting app like Emma, Money Dashboard, or YNAB. Or go old school with a spreadsheet or notebook.

Step 3: Assign Every Pound a Job

This is the key difference between tracking and budgeting.

It's not enough to *look* at your spending, you need to *plan* it.

Give every pound a purpose:

    Save it

    Spend it intentionally

    Invest it

    Use it to pay off debt

✅ *Tip:* Use the "zero-based budgeting" method, where your income minus expenses equals zero, because every pound is *assigned*, not wasted.

Clarity Beats Willpower Every Time

You don't need to be more disciplined. You need to be more *clear*.

Willpower is fickle. It fades when you're tired, stressed, or tempted.

But **clarity creates automatic confidence**.

When you know exactly where your money's going, you make better decisions *without thinking*. You don't need to fight temptation, you've already made the decision in advance.

Clarity gives you permission to spend *without guilt*. If it's in the budget, you're good. If it's not, you pause and reconsider. It's that simple.

Budgeting isn't about being perfect. It's about being *aware*.

Real Story: Amelia Finds £500/Month by Plugging the Leaks

Let's go back to Amelia.

She's a 31-year-old administrator in Bristol, earning £26,000 a year. Every month felt like a struggle. Her credit card balance hovered around £4,000, and she couldn't figure out why she wasn't making progress.

One afternoon, she sat down and pulled her bank statements from the past three months.

Here's what she discovered:

£220/month on eating out and takeaway coffee

£65/month on forgotten subscriptions

£120/month on impulse Amazon purchases

£100/month in contactless card charges she couldn't even remember

Total: **£505/month**, on autopilot.

She didn't cancel everything overnight. But she did make changes:

Started meal prepping and bringing a flask to work

Cancelled unused subscriptions

Set a £50/month Amazon cap

Switched to using cash for discretionary spending

Six months later:

Credit card balance: **£0**

Emergency fund: **£1,200**

Peace of mind: *priceless*

She didn't earn more. She didn't "hustle." She just stopped letting money leak out.

And now? She uses a simple Google Sheet to track her income and expenses, and feels more in control than ever.

Your Wealth-Building Action for This Chapter

Ready to reclaim your money?

Here's your 7-day challenge:

Track Every Pound You Spend for One Week

Use an app, notebook, or spreadsheet, just write it all down.

Be honest, not perfect. Awareness is the goal.

Categorise It

Label each expense: Essential, Fixed, or Discretionary.

> See where your money *wants* to go, and where you want to *redirect* it.

Find Your Leaks

> Highlight anything that doesn't reflect your values or goals.
>
> Choose one area to reduce *this week*, not later.

Create a "First Budget" for Next Month

> Use your tracking data to make your first plan.
>
> Assign every pound a job, even if the numbers aren't perfect yet.

✓ *Bonus:* Schedule a 30-minute "money meeting" with yourself once a week. Look at your progress, adjust, and celebrate small wins.

Takeaway: Tracking Is the First Step to Transformation

Most people don't have a money problem, they have a *clarity* problem.

When you track your spending, you'll find:

    Hidden cash flow you didn't know existed

    Decisions that once felt hard become easy

    Guilt and anxiety replaced by confidence and control

You don't need to wait for a raise to get ahead.
You just need to *know where your money is going, and tell it where to go next.*

So grab your bank statement. Open that spreadsheet. Start tracking.

Because every pound you track is a pound you take back.

Chapter 4: Paying Yourself First, No Matter How Small

Callum used to do what most people do with his paycheque.

He paid the rent. Covered the bills. Bought groceries. Picked up a few things online. Went out on the weekend. And *then*, if anything was left at the end of the month, he'd try to save.

Most months, nothing was left.

It wasn't that Callum was irresponsible, he was careful, even frugal. But somehow, saving always came last. A "nice idea" rather than a non-negotiable.

That changed the day a friend told him:
 "You don't save what's left over. You save first, or not at all."

Callum took that advice to heart. He set up an automatic transfer of £20 a month to a separate savings account. Not much. But it was consistent.

Two years later, he was saving over £500 a month.
 Same salary. Different system.
 Different mindset. Different results.

And it all started with one simple shift: **paying himself first.**

Why Saving First Matters More Than How Much

Let's get something clear from the start.

The *amount* you save matters, but it matters **less** than the *habit* of saving consistently.

When you pay yourself first:

>You prioritise your future over your impulses.

>You treat saving as essential, not optional.

>You build momentum, even if it starts small.

Most people treat savings like leftovers. But here's the truth:

>**If you wait until the end of the month to save, there'll rarely be anything left.**

Why?

Because life expands to fill your budget. There's always another dinner out, another sale, another unexpected expense. If savings aren't automated and protected, they vanish.

But when you pay yourself first, automatically, off the top, you flip the script. You *force* your spending to adjust to what's left over. And somehow, it always does.

This single decision, done consistently, can change your entire financial future.

Automate to Eliminate Excuses

Saving manually sounds nice in theory. But it's fragile.

You *mean* to transfer money. You *intend* to put some aside. But life gets busy. Temptation strikes. Things come up.

That's why wealthy people automate.

They know that willpower is unreliable, but automation is bulletproof.

Here's how to do it:

Step 1: Open a Separate Account

Choose a high-interest savings account or a stocks and shares ISA, somewhere you won't accidentally dip into it.

Step 2: Set Up an Automatic Transfer

As soon as your paycheque lands, have a set amount automatically moved to your savings or investment account.

Start with as little as £10 or £20 a month.

Date the transfer to hit the day *after* payday.

Step 3: Forget It's There

Seriously. Don't obsess. Let it grow in the background. Check in once a month, not once an hour.

✓ *Pro tip:* Give your savings account a name that reminds you of your goal, like "Freedom Fund" or "Future Me."

Start Small, Build Momentum

You don't need to start big. You just need to **start**.

What matters most in wealth-building is **momentum**. Even £10 a month builds the muscle. It shifts your identity. It changes how you think.

Here's the magic:

£20/month saved = £240/year

£50/month invested = £600/year + potential compound growth

£100/month over 10 years = £12,000 + thousands in interest

Now imagine increasing that amount slowly every few months. A little raise here. A few cutbacks there. Before you know it, you're saving hundreds without feeling the squeeze.

Wealth isn't built in one giant leap, it's built in quiet, repeated steps.

Real Story: From £20 to £500/Month, Callum's Journey

Callum works in a warehouse in Leeds. He started on £19,500/year and now earns about £24,000. Not a huge salary. No inheritance. No business on the side.

But he made a powerful decision two years ago: pay himself first.

He began with £20/month into a savings account. It felt symbolic more than significant, but he did it every month without fail.

After six months, he bumped it to £40. Then £75. He cancelled unused subscriptions, cooked at home more often, and took on occasional overtime shifts.

By the end of year one, he was saving £200/month.
By the end of year two, it was £500/month, including £100 into a stocks and shares ISA and £50 into a pension top-up.

His total savings? Just over **£7,800**.

The best part? He never felt like he was "cutting back", because every increase in savings came from changes he *chose*, not sacrifices he resented.

Now, Callum sees himself as someone who *builds wealth*.
And it all started with a single £20 transfer.

Why This Works on Any Income

People often say, *"I'll start saving when I earn more."*
But the truth is: **you can't save more later if you don't practise saving now.**

Every pound saved is a signal:

> To your brain: "This is who I am."

To your habits: "This is what I do."

To your future: "I've got your back."

Saving £10 might not change your life today. But doing it **every month for five years**, increasing slowly, *absolutely will.*

Your Wealth-Building Action for This Chapter

Let's set up your first step.

Open a Separate "Pay Yourself First" Account

High-interest savings or investment platform, just don't link it to your spending account.

Set Up an Automatic Transfer

Pick a number that feels *easy* to start, £10, £20, or £50.

Date it for the day after payday.

Make a Plan to Increase Over Time

Add a calendar reminder every 3 months to review and increase the amount, by even just £5.

Celebrate the Habit, Not Just the Number

Track your savings growth. Watch how it changes *you*, not just your balance.

Takeaway: You Are Your First and Most Important Bill

Before you pay anyone else, your landlord, your phone company, the supermarket, **pay yourself**.

You work hard. You show up. You give your time, your energy, your life. You deserve to keep a portion of that.

Not someday. Not when you get a raise. But *now*.

Wealth doesn't start with a salary. It starts with a decision:

"From this month forward, I pay myself first."

Let that decision compound. Let that £10 become £100. Let that habit become who you are.

Because the only thing better than earning money, is knowing that some of it is staying with you.

Chapter 5: Slashing Lifestyle Inflation

When Emma and James graduated from university, they were used to sharing meals, cycling to work, and splitting rent with friends. Their total combined income? Just under £28,000.

Five years later, both had steady careers, Emma as a secondary school teacher, James in IT support. Their combined income had jumped to £40,000. A comfortable increase.

But something interesting happened.
They didn't change their lifestyle.

They kept renting their modest two-bedroom flat.
They meal-prepped every Sunday like they used to.
They still rode bikes instead of upgrading to a car.
They chose picnics and game nights over expensive evenings out.

Fast forward six years: they'd saved over £60,000, invested another £25,000, and were in the process of buying their first home, with a 30% deposit.

Their secret? They ignored the urge to "upgrade."

They didn't let their expenses rise just because their income had.

That decision is what separates *comfortable spenders* from *wealth builders*.

Why Most Raises Disappear Overnight

If you've ever received a raise and felt like it vanished the next day, you're not alone. It's not bad maths, it's lifestyle inflation.

Lifestyle inflation is what happens when your spending increases the moment your income does. More dinners out. A new car. Upgraded clothes. Fancy coffee every day instead of once a week.

It's not that you *mean* to spend more, it just... happens.

Suddenly, the paycheque that was supposed to change your life feels exactly like the old one. Except now, your expenses are bigger and your habits are harder to break.

And here's the dangerous part: lifestyle inflation feels *normal*. Society encourages it. Marketers expect it. Your peers are doing it.

But if you want to build wealth, real, lasting wealth, you have to be *intentional*. Because raises without discipline don't lead to freedom. They lead to faster treadmills.

Avoiding "Upgrade Syndrome"

"Upgrade syndrome" is sneaky. It's the feeling that every life improvement *must* be matched with a financial one.

New job? You *deserve* a nicer flat.
Promotion? Time for that new iPhone.
Bonus? Let's book that luxury holiday.

But here's the truth:

> **Just because you *can* afford something doesn't mean you should.**

There's nothing wrong with treating yourself now and then. The problem arises when every financial gain triggers a lifestyle upgrade.

Wealth builders take a different approach. They *pause*. They *plan*. They let their financial future, not their ego, guide their spending.

Here's a question that can stop upgrade syndrome in its tracks:

> *"If I didn't know I had more money, would I still buy this?"*

If the answer is no, it's not a need. It's a reaction.

How to Keep Expenses Steady While Income Rises

Here's the secret formula wealthy people use:

Freeze your lifestyle. Invest the raise.

Every time your income increases, whether it's a raise, bonus, or new job, resist the urge to increase your spending proportionally.

Instead, do this:

Decide your current lifestyle is "enough"

> Be intentional. Write down what's "good enough" for your housing, transport, food, etc.

Split raises into buckets

> 50% toward long-term goals (investing, saving, debt repayment)
>
> 30% to boost future security (emergency fund, pension)
>
> 20% to spend on fun, *guilt-free*

Create a "Future Fund"

Use pay rises to fund your goals, not your lifestyle. Label it. Track it. Celebrate progress.

Review spending annually, not emotionally

Make upgrades intentional and rare, not reactive and constant.

✓ *Pro tip:* Pretend you never got the raise. Increase your standing orders to savings or investments the same month it lands.

Key Insight: Living Below Your Means Is the Wealth Superpower

Everyone wants a financial edge. Some look for high-paying careers. Others chase the next investment trend. But the most underrated, timeless advantage is this:

Living below your means, consistently, is the ultimate wealth-building habit.

It protects you during downturns.
It creates surplus for saving and investing.
It reduces stress, debt, and dependency.
It gives you freedom far earlier than your peers.

Living below your means isn't about being stingy. It's about **choosing freedom over flash.**

Real Story: Emma and James, Student Budget, Wealthy Future

Emma and James, the couple from earlier, decided early on that *more income didn't mean more spending*. They remembered how little they lived on at university and made a simple decision:
Let's keep living like students, even if we're not anymore.

Here's what they did:

- Continued meal prepping and buying food in bulk
- Took UK-based budget holidays instead of flying abroad
- Rented a modest flat in a less trendy area
- Delayed car ownership in favour of cycling and public transport
- Set up standing orders to auto-invest 20% of their combined income

Result?

By the time they were earning £40,000/year combined, they were saving and investing over £800/month.

They built an emergency fund, opened a Lifetime ISA each, and contributed to pensions.

While friends talked about how "tight" money felt, Emma and James quietly built financial peace.

They didn't deprive themselves, they just defined success differently.

Now, they're on track to retire a decade earlier than most.

Your Wealth-Building Action for This Chapter

It's time to tame lifestyle inflation and turn raises into freedom.

Review the Last Raise You Got

What changed after you earned more?

Did you upgrade anything, housing, transport, habits?

Define Your Baseline Lifestyle

Write down what's "enough" for now. Housing, clothes, food, fun.

Let that be your benchmark, not your peers or Pinterest.

Create a Raise Plan

Next time you earn more, how will you allocate it?

Set percentages *now* so you don't fall into reactive spending later.

Start the "Freeze and Grow" Challenge

Freeze your lifestyle for the next 6–12 months.

Commit to investing or saving 100% of any pay increase in that time.

✓ *Bonus:* Set calendar reminders to check in with yourself every 3 months. Adjust with intention, not impulse.

Takeaway: The Richest People Don't Look Rich

You can spend your raises on upgrades, or you can spend them on your future.

One brings momentary status.
The other brings lasting peace.

You don't need to live like a monk or deny yourself forever. But if you can live like a student a little longer, you'll live like a millionaire much sooner.

So the next time more money comes in, ask yourself:

> *"Will I use this to look richer, or to actually be richer?"*

That one question could change your entire financial life.

Chapter 6: Building an Emergency Fund on Any Income

Maya worked in a café earning minimum wage. Her shifts varied week to week, and there were months she barely scraped together enough to cover rent and travel. Saving felt like a distant luxury, something "for later."

But after a boiler breakdown left her relying on a high-interest credit card she couldn't immediately pay off, she realised something important:

Emergencies don't wait for perfect timing.

So Maya made a choice. Not to earn more overnight. Not to magically eliminate expenses. But to build a financial buffer, *no matter how small she had to start*.

One year later, she had over **£1,000 saved**.
 Same job. Same rent. Same hourly wage.
 Different mindset. Different future.

Her story proves a powerful truth:
 Emergency funds aren't just for the wealthy, they're the reason many people *become* wealthy.

Why Emergency Savings Matter More Than You Think

Picture your financial goals like a house.

> Your **income** is the materials, what you're working with.
>
> Your **budget** is the blueprint.
>
> Your **investments** are the growth, the expansion.
>
> But your **emergency fund**? That's the *foundation*.

Without it, everything else is shaky.

Because life happens. Fridges break. Shifts get cancelled. Kids get sick. And when you don't have a buffer, your only option is often **debt**.

Debt creates cycles.
Cycles kill momentum.
And momentum is the lifeblood of wealth building.

A well-funded emergency fund gives you:

> **Peace of mind**, knowing you can handle surprises
>
> **Protection**, against taking on expensive debt
>
> **Power**, to say no to bad jobs, bad landlords, or bad relationships

It doesn't just keep you *safe*. It keeps you *free*.

How to Save, Even on a Tight Budget

Let's address the elephant in the room: saving when money's already tight feels impossible.

But here's the good news, you don't need to stash thousands to start. The goal isn't perfection. The goal is progress.

Here's how to begin, even on a minimum wage or unpredictable income:

1. Start with Micro-Savings

Even £5/week matters. It's the *habit* that counts. Use apps like Monzo, Starling, or Plum to automate round-ups or micro-transfers every time you spend.

2. Use the "First Pound" Rule

Pay yourself *first*, even if it's just £1. Prove to yourself that saving is non-negotiable.

3. Create a "No-Spend" Challenge

Pick one weekend or one category (e.g., no takeaway this month) and direct the saved cash straight into your fund.

4. Reclaim Hidden Money

Audit your bank statements. Cancel unused subscriptions. Sell something you haven't touched in a year. Shift to value brands. All that adds up fast.

✓ *Pro tip:* Open a savings account at a separate bank, make it slightly harder to access. Label it "Safety Net" or "Freedom Fund."

Creative Ways to Jumpstart Your Fund

If you're truly at your limit with your current income, here are low-barrier ways to generate an emergency stash without taking on another full job:

1. Offer Simple Services

Pet-sitting, house-cleaning, ironing, tutoring, admin help, whatever's in demand locally.

2. Sell Time, Not Products

Busy people pay for convenience. You can run errands, wait in queues, assemble flat-pack furniture.

3. Resell What You Already Own

Old phones, unused clothes, books, tech, Facebook Marketplace, Vinted, Gumtree.

4. Turn Hobbies into Micro-Gigs

Are you good at drawing, proofreading, or photography? Someone needs what you do. Start small. Start locally.

Your first £100 might take effort. But your next £100 will take *less*. Because momentum breeds confidence.

Key Insight: Security First, Growth Second

It's easy to get caught up in the excitement of investing, side hustles, or smashing goals. But **none of it works if you're one emergency away from disaster.**

That's why:

> Before you invest, build your buffer.
>
> Before you scale, secure the basics.
>
> Before you chase "more", protect what you already have.

Financial security isn't boring. It's brave. It's smart. It's step one.

And it's *doable*, even on a low income.

Real Story: Maya's £1,000 Emergency Fund on Minimum Wage

Maya, the barista from earlier, was earning just under £11/hour on a zero-hours contract in Liverpool. Her rent took up over half her pay. She often dipped into her overdraft just to get by.

After her boiler fiasco and the panic that followed, she set one simple goal: **build a £500 emergency fund in one year.**

Here's what she did:

> She opened a second savings account and nicknamed it "Safety Net."
>
> She started transferring £5/week, no matter what.
>
> She cut takeaway coffees (ironically) and brought her own lunch, saving around £60/month.
>
> She sold old clothes and a tablet she never used, raising £200.
>
> She found a Saturday cleaning job for £40/week and directed *all* of it into her fund.

By month 8, she'd hit her £500 goal. By month 14, she passed £1,000.

More than the money, it was what it *meant* to her:

> She no longer feared unexpected expenses.
>
> She stopped relying on credit.
>
> She began to see herself not as "broke," but as "building."

That mental shift fuelled her next steps, paying off debt and investing for the first time.

All from £5 at a time.

Your Wealth-Building Action for This Chapter

Let's take action, right now, from where you are.

Set Your First Emergency Fund Goal

> Aim for £500 to start. It's achievable and impactful.

Open a Dedicated "Safety Net" Account

Not for holidays. Not for shopping. This is for life's curveballs.

Choose Your Starting Contribution

Can you spare £5/week? £10/month? Automate it today.

Find One Cash Flow Boost This Week

Sell one item, cancel one subscription, take one micro-job, and transfer the proceeds.

Make It Visible

Track your progress on paper or with an app. Celebrate small milestones.

✅ *Bonus:* Share your goal with someone you trust. Accountability keeps momentum alive.

Takeaway: Peace of Mind Is Priceless

You don't need £5,000 to feel safe. You don't need a perfect income to create a buffer.

You just need:

A clear goal

A system to start

The courage to prioritise security

Wealth isn't built on risk alone. It's built on a stable foundation.

And nothing says "I'm in control" like knowing you could handle a surprise expense *without panic*.

So protect yourself. Build your buffer. And let that safety net become your launch pad to greater freedom.

Chapter 7: Killing Consumer Debt Fast

When Jordan finally sat down and added up his debts, he felt sick.

Three credit cards. An overdraft. A car loan. A few "buy now, pay later" instalments he'd lost track of. Total consumer debt: **£15,207**.

Jordan wasn't reckless, he was just like so many others trying to get by. The debt hadn't come from shopping sprees or designer labels. It had crept up through emergencies, rent gaps, and small short-term decisions that snowballed.

He was earning £26,000 a year working in IT support. And every month, hundreds of pounds were vanishing into minimum payments.

He wasn't building wealth, he was barely treading water.

That's when something clicked.

He realised:
 Every pound he sent to debt was a pound he couldn't use to invest, save, or move forward.

And so, with no fancy income or miracle windfall, Jordan made a plan, and in just under three years, he paid off every penny.

His story isn't rare because of the amount. It's rare because he stuck with it.

And it starts with one powerful truth:

> **You can't build real wealth until you stop bleeding money into consumer debt.**

Why Debt Sabotages Wealth Growth

Let's be honest, consumer debt is one of the biggest barriers to financial freedom. It steals your money, your momentum, and your peace of mind.

Here's how it quietly destroys your wealth:

> **High interest eats future income.**
> A £3,000 balance at 20% APR, with only minimum payments, could cost you **£1,600+** in interest alone, and take years to clear.
>
> **Minimum payments keep you stuck.**
> They make it feel manageable, but they're designed to *maximise profit* for the lender, not help you escape.
>
> **Debt delays progress.**
> You can't invest, save, or grow if you're using tomorrow's income to pay for yesterday's

choices.

It creates mental clutter.
Financial anxiety drains your energy. Even small debts can feel like a weight on your shoulders.

That's why killing consumer debt isn't just about the maths. It's about *momentum*. When you remove that drag, everything else accelerates.

The Two Fastest Ways to Pay Off Debt: Snowball vs Avalanche

There's no one-size-fits-all debt payoff method, but there *is* a method that fits *you*.

Let's break down the two most popular strategies.

1. The Debt Snowball (Best for Motivation)

List debts from smallest to largest, regardless of interest rate.

Make minimum payments on all debts.

Throw any extra money at the *smallest* debt first.

Once it's paid off, roll that payment into the next smallest.

Why it works:
Quick wins fuel motivation. You feel progress faster, and that keeps you going.

✓ *Best for:* People who need emotional wins to stay committed.

2. The Debt Avalanche (Best for Efficiency)

List debts from highest to lowest interest rate.

Make minimum payments on all.

Focus all extra money on the *highest interest* debt first.

Why it works:
You pay less interest overall. It's the mathematically optimal route.

✓ *Best for:* People motivated by numbers and long-term savings.

Whichever you choose, pick one and commit.
The best method is the one you actually follow.

How to Stay Motivated While Paying Off Debt

Paying off debt isn't glamorous. It's repetitive. Slow. Quiet. And some days it feels like you're not getting anywhere.

But here's how you stay fired up:

1. Visualise Your Freedom

Create a debt tracker. Colour it in. Watch the balance drop. Celebrate each milestone.

2. Name Your "Why"

Debt freedom isn't the goal. It's the gateway. What will being debt-free allow you to do? Travel? Save for a house? Sleep better?

3. Create a Mini-Reward System

Set markers, £1,000 paid off, next card cleared, and treat yourself in a small, intentional way.

4. Find an Accountability Partner

Share your goal with a friend or join a free online money group. Momentum grows in community.

5. Reframe the Hard Days

Every time you make a payment, tell yourself:

> *"I'm buying back my future. One pound at a time."*

Real Story: Jordan Pays Off £15,000 on a Modest Income

Let's go back to Jordan.

At 27, he was working full time and earning £26,000. His £15,207 debt wasn't from wild spending, it was from life.

But once he committed to becoming debt-free, here's what he did:

- He chose the **debt snowball** method to keep himself motivated.

- He paused all non-essential spending, cancelling subscriptions, cycling instead of driving, meal-prepping every week.

- He picked up small freelance gigs doing IT setup for local businesses, adding £150–£200/month to his income.

- He built a spreadsheet tracker and checked it weekly. He celebrated every £1,000 milestone with a night in and a homemade pizza.

He channelled all "found money" (gifts, tax refunds, side income) straight to debt.

Some months were hard. Really hard. But after **32 months**, every balance read £0.

More importantly?

His credit score improved dramatically.

He began saving £300/month immediately.

He finally opened an ISA and started investing.

And for the first time in years, he felt *light*.

Key Insight: Every Pound of Debt Paid Is a Pound Freed to Build Wealth

Think of it like this:

When you pay your credit card, that £50 payment *doesn't come back*.

But once the debt is gone, that £50 is *yours to keep*. To save. To invest. To use for freedom.

Debt keeps your money chained to the past.
Paying it off sets it free, to work for your *future*.

Every pound you pay off:

>Reduces your monthly obligations

>Increases your flexibility

>Builds financial confidence

It's not just debt reduction, it's **wealth recovery**.

Your Wealth-Building Action for This Chapter

Time to create your personal debt-freedom plan.

List All Your Debts

>Include balance, minimum payment, and interest rate.

Choose Your Method

Snowball: Smallest to largest.

Avalanche: Highest interest to lowest.

Set a Monthly Target

How much *extra* can you throw at your target debt? Even £20 makes a difference.

Automate Your Plan

Schedule payments immediately after payday, remove temptation.

Create a Victory Chart

Track your progress visually. Make it fun. Make it real.

✓ *Bonus:* Pick one "found money" challenge this month, sell an item, skip a night out, or take a micro-gig. Send 100% of that to debt.

Takeaway: Kill Debt, Reclaim Your Future

You are not your debt.
* You are not stuck.
You are not behind.

You are on the path to freedom, one pound at a time.

And every pound of consumer debt you kill is a pound you set free.
 To grow.
 To build.
 To become the wealth you're meant to hold.

So sharpen your plan. Stick with it. And celebrate the smallest wins, because they lead to the biggest changes.

This is your turning point.

Chapter 8: Automating Wealth-Building Habits

Rachel never considered herself "good with money." She hated budgeting, struggled with discipline, and found it hard to stay consistent. Every month, she'd resolve to save more, track her spending, or invest a little, but life always got in the way.

Then one day, she heard a phrase that changed her approach entirely:

"You don't need more discipline. You need fewer decisions."

So she set up a simple system:

> £100 transferred automatically to savings the day after payday.

> £50 invested into a stocks and shares ISA.

> Her credit card paid down on direct debit.

> Bills and rent scheduled to come out early in the month.

She stopped trying to *remember* to build wealth, and started letting her systems do it for her.

Twelve months later, she had saved **£2,400**, invested **£600**, and cleared a lingering balance on her card.

No hustle. No spreadsheets. No stress.
Just a system that ran quietly in the background while she lived her life.

And that's the power of automation.

Why Automation Is Your Financial Superpower

Wealth isn't built by force of will, it's built by the right systems.

The truth is, most of us don't have a money *knowledge* problem. We know we should save. We know we should pay down debt. We've read the books, listened to the podcasts, nodded along to the advice.

The problem is *consistency*.

That's where automation comes in.

> **Automation takes willpower out of the equation.**
> **It turns good intentions into guaranteed action.**

Because let's face it: life gets busy. Motivation dips. Emergencies pop up. But if your system is already working in the background, wealth still gets built, even when you're distracted, tired, or stressed.

And over time, those quiet, automated moves compound into something powerful.

The "Set It and Forget It" Approach to Wealth

Let's break down how to automate the three key pillars of wealth-building:

1. Automate Your Savings

Why it matters:
If you wait until the end of the month to save, it won't happen. When you automate savings from the top, you force yourself to live on what's left, and somehow, you do.

How to do it:

- Open a separate high-interest savings account.

- Set up a standing order for a fixed amount to transfer *the day after payday*.

Start small, £20, £50, £100. Increase over time.

✓ *Pro tip:* Rename your account something meaningful, "Emergency Fund," "Freedom Fund," or "Holiday Cash."

---

2. Automate Your Investments

Why it matters:
Investing regularly, even in small amounts, is how long-term wealth is built. Automation removes the "should I invest this month?" question.

How to do it:

> Use an investing platform or app that supports monthly contributions (e.g., Moneybox, Vanguard, Nutmeg).
>
> Choose a simple product like a stocks and shares ISA with an index fund.
>
> Set up a direct debit to invest automatically every month.

✓ *Pro tip:* Automate a small amount now, even if it's £25/month. You can always increase it later.

3. Automate Your Debt Payments

Why it matters:
Missed or late payments cost money, and motivation. Automation keeps your payoff plan on track.

How to do it:

Set up direct debits for all minimum payments.

Add a scheduled overpayment on your target debt (based on the snowball or avalanche method from Chapter 7).

Link payments to payday timing to avoid shortfalls.

✅ *Pro tip:* If your income varies, set payment dates a few days after payday to avoid overdraft charges.

How Automation Removes Temptation and Friction

Temptation thrives in gaps. Gaps between intent and action.

"I'll transfer that money later…"

"I'll invest after I buy this…"

"I'll pay more on the card next month…"

Automation removes the gap.

It eliminates the chance for emotion, impulse, or forgetfulness to hijack your goals. It makes wealth-building the default.

Even better? Once you see progress happening without stress, you start to trust the process, and your financial identity begins to shift.

You stop feeling like someone who *tries* to build wealth. You become someone who *does*.

Real Story: Rachel's Wealth Built on Autopilot

Rachel, the admin assistant from earlier, never saw herself as "a saver." She earned £23,000 working at a university and had struggled for years to stick to any financial habit.

But after hearing about automation in a podcast, she decided to try it.

Here's her setup:

> £100/month to savings, every payday.
>
> £50/month to a stocks and shares ISA.
>
> £150/month to her credit card (minimum + extra).
>
> Bills all set up to run within the first five days of the month.

She never touched that money. It just moved, quietly, reliably.

Here's what changed in a year:

> Emergency fund: £1,400
>
> Investment account: £600
>
> Credit card balance: £0
>
> Stress level: *way* down

She didn't work more hours. She didn't master budgeting.
 She just took her goals off the to-do list and put them on autopilot.

Now, Rachel feels in control. And that confidence is spilling into other areas of her life, asking for a raise, planning holidays, and dreaming bigger.

It all started with one standing order.

Key Insight: Automation Builds Wealth When Motivation Fades

Let's be honest, motivation is fickle.

You might feel fired up after reading a book, attending a workshop, or listening to a podcast. But that energy fades.

Automation is your financial backup plan.
It protects you from yourself.
It makes doing the right thing *easier than doing nothing.*

Think of it like brushing your teeth. You don't need to be inspired, you just do it. Daily discipline becomes second nature.

And over time, those automated choices create an outcome that feels like magic, but was really just maths and momentum.

Your Wealth-Building Action for This Chapter

Let's make your money move, even when you don't.

Pick One Area to Automate This Week

> Savings, investing, or debt payment, choose one.
>
> Set up a standing order or direct debit today.

Set the Date

> Line it up with payday. Make the action happen before you even notice the money.

Name Your Goal

> Give the account a label that makes it real, something meaningful and personal.

Review in 3 Months

> Set a reminder to revisit and increase the amount. But until then, don't tinker. Let it run.

✅ *Bonus:* Write yourself a note: *"Wealth is being built, even when I'm not thinking about it."*

Stick it near your desk, mirror, or phone background.

Takeaway: Systems Build Success, Not Willpower

The richest people don't rely on motivation. They rely on *systems*.
They know that effort fades, but structure lasts.

So stop trying to remember. Stop trying to do it all manually.
Let the tech work for you. Let the system carry the weight.
And let your future self enjoy the results.

Because when you automate your habits, you don't just build wealth.

You build a life where wealth is the *default*.

Chapter 9: Growing Income Strategically

Amy was a secondary school English teacher in Sheffield. She earned £32,000 a year and was already living frugally, packed lunches, no car, holidaying in the UK. She tracked her spending, avoided debt, and paid herself first.

But despite doing *everything right*, her savings were growing slowly. She wanted to build wealth faster, but cutting more wasn't the answer.

So she flipped the script.

Amy began offering one-on-one tutoring sessions from home two evenings a week. Just an hour or two each night. Within three months, she was earning **an extra £500/month.**

That's **£6,000 a year**, nearly a 20% raise without changing jobs.

And every pound of that side income went straight into her investments and house deposit savings.

Her lifestyle didn't change. But her trajectory did.

This chapter is about unlocking *that* kind of growth, not through exhaustion, but through strategy.

Why Cutting Expenses Alone Isn't Enough

You've probably heard the advice: *"Just stop buying coffee."*
But here's the truth:

You can't shrink your way to wealth.

Yes, living below your means is essential. Budgeting matters. But there's a ceiling to how much you can cut, and no ceiling to how much you can earn.

At a certain point, especially on modest incomes, cutting more simply becomes unsustainable. That's when it's time to look at the other side of the equation:

Don't just manage your money, grow it.

The fastest way to accelerate wealth?
Increase your income and keep your lifestyle steady.
That gap between what you earn and what you spend? That's where wealth is born.

How to Increase Your Income on the Side

You don't need to start a company or become an influencer. You just need to look at your existing time, skills, and interests, and match them with *market demand*.

Here are accessible ways to grow your income without burning out:

1. Freelancing (Online or Local)

> Writing, design, admin support, proofreading, editing
>
> Use platforms like Fiverr, Upwork, or local Facebook groups

> ✓ *Example:* Someone who writes resumes or cover letters for £40 a pop can earn £400+ a month from just 10 clients.

2. Tutoring or Teaching

> Academic subjects, music, languages, tech skills
>
> Sites like Tutorful, Superprof, or even Zoom and word-of-mouth

> ✓ *Best for:* Teachers, university students, professionals with niche skills

3. Gig Economy Platforms

Deliveroo, Uber Eats, TaskRabbit, pet-sitting via Rover

✓ *Warning:* These work best short-term. Great for quick cash but harder to scale long-term.

4. Sell What You Know or Create

Ebooks, guides, templates, online courses, Etsy crafts

✓ *Best for:* Creatives or anyone with a "how to" skill they can teach or design

5. Certifications That Pay Off

Short-term upskilling: digital marketing, bookkeeping, project management

Free or low-cost courses from platforms like Coursera, FutureLearn, Google Digital Garage

✓ *Think long game:* Some £100–£300 courses can lead to £5,000+ pay bumps.

Leveraging Existing Skills for Higher Earnings

You don't always need to *add* new skills, you might already be sitting on untapped earning potential.

Ask yourself:

> What do people already ask me for help with?
>
> What problems do I naturally solve?
>
> What have I done professionally that others might pay to learn?

Sometimes, it's about repositioning what you already do.

> Are you organised? Offer virtual assistant services.
>
> Good with spreadsheets? Help small businesses with basic bookkeeping.
>
> Love kids? Babysit or tutor part-time.
>
> Tech-savvy? Help older people set up devices or use apps.

You don't need a new career. You need a *sharper lens*.

Key Insight: You Don't Need a Second Job, You Need a Smarter Income Plan

Too many people hear "earn more" and picture working double shifts and exhausting themselves.

But this is about being strategic, not sacrificial.

Instead of:

> "How can I work more hours?"

Ask:

> "How can I earn more from the hours I already have?"
> "How can I use my skills to create extra value?"
> "How can I make my money grow *without* burning out?"

This is about **return on energy**, not just effort.

And it starts by being *intentional*, not reactive.

Real Story: Amy's £500/Month Tutoring Side Hustle

Back to Amy, the English teacher from Sheffield.

She didn't want to burn out. Teaching already took a lot of energy.

But she realised there was a high demand for private tutoring, especially in the run-up to GCSE and A-Level exams.

She began offering tutoring two nights a week from 6:30–8:30pm, charging £25/hour. Within weeks, her slots were full, mostly from word-of-mouth referrals.

Here's what changed in a year:

>Extra income: **£6,000+**
>
>House deposit savings: grew from £3,200 to over **£10,000**
>
>Confidence: through the roof
>
>Lifestyle: unchanged, she still took the same holidays and lived modestly

What started as a side hustle soon became her fast-track to financial freedom.

Your Wealth-Building Action for This Chapter

Time to put a smart income strategy in motion.

List Your Marketable Skills

What do you know how to do? What do people compliment you on?

Choose a Simple Monetisation Path

Tutoring, freelancing, gig work, product creation, pick one to try for 30 days.

Create a Low-Bar Entry Plan

Don't overthink it. One client. One project. One evening a week. That's it.

Ring-Fence the Earnings

Don't let extra income blend into daily spending. Create a separate account and *assign that money a mission*, savings, debt, investment.

✓ *Bonus:* Track your hourly ROI. If you earn £25/hour doing tutoring or freelance work, compare that to other options. Use your energy where it pays best.

Takeaway: Your Skills Are Seeds, Plant Them Wisely

You don't need to win the lottery or land a dream job to grow your income.

You need to:

    Use what you already know

    Package it with intention

    Focus your energy where it pays best

    Keep your lifestyle steady while your income rises

That's how you create a *wealth gap*, not just an income spike.

So ask yourself:

> *"What skill do I already have that could earn me £250 this month?"*

Start there. Grow from there. And let your income become your rocket fuel.

Chapter 10: Avoiding the Big Money Traps

Tariq was earning £22,000 a year working in retail. He wasn't extravagant, just trying to live a little. Nights out with mates. Takeaway Fridays. A few "small" Klarna purchases to replace clothes that were "getting tired."

But by the end of each month, he was scraping by, dipping into his overdraft and occasionally using payday loans "just to tide him over."

One evening, after racking up a new £300 clothing bill on buy-now-pay-later, he sat down and did the maths.

Over the past year, he'd paid:

£580 in overdraft fees

£230 in late Klarna payments

£480 in impulse purchases

£150 on subscriptions he'd forgotten about

Total: **£1,440**, *gone*. Not on purpose. Not on luxury. Just… gone.

That night, Tariq made a decision: no more traps.

He cancelled subscriptions. Unlinked his card from shopping apps. Said no to peer pressure weekends. And in 12 months, he flipped that £1,440 drain into £2,000 saved.

The lesson?

> **Avoiding the wrong moves matters just as much as making the right ones.**

The Hidden Ways Small Incomes Stay Stuck

If you're living on a modest income, the margin for error is small. Just a few "harmless" habits can quietly sabotage your progress.

Let's expose the most common traps keeping earners stuck.

1. Payday Loans and High-Cost Credit

- Short-term loans with extortionate APRs (often 300%+).

- Promise fast cash, but deliver long-term pain.

- One missed payment = snowballing debt.

✓ *Better option:* Build a micro emergency fund. Use credit unions or community lenders if absolutely necessary.

2. Subscription Creep

Gym memberships, streaming platforms, apps, delivery passes.

Many start "free" or cheap, then never get cancelled.

£7.99 here, £4.99 there… adds up to hundreds a year.

✓ *Audit action:* Review all automatic payments every three months.

3. Buy Now, Pay Later Schemes

Klarna, Clearpay, Laybuy, designed to *feel* painless.

Break up the payment, break down your discipline.

Encourages overspending on things you don't actually need.

✓ *Rule of thumb:* If you can't buy it in full without stress, you can't afford it.

4. Emotional or Retail Therapy

Buying things to feel better, when stressed, bored, or down.

Quick dopamine, long-term regret.

Often targets the same areas: clothes, gadgets, takeaways.

✓ *Alternative:* Create a "cooling off" list, if you want something, wait 72 hours before deciding.

Saying No to "Keeping Up Appearances"

Social pressure is one of the most powerful (and invisible) money traps.

You know the feeling:

Everyone's chipping in for a pricey dinner, and you don't want to be *that* person.

Your friends are booking city breaks, while you're barely affording rent.

Someone raises an eyebrow when you say you're saving money.

But here's the truth:

You don't owe anyone a performance of wealth.

If someone makes you feel small for living within your means, they're not a friend, they're a distraction.

Saying "no" to things you can't afford isn't weakness. It's *wisdom*. It's strength. It's wealth in action.

And the people who truly care about you? They'll respect your boundaries. Or better yet, be inspired by them.

Practising Conscious Consumption

Being frugal doesn't mean being stingy. It means being **deliberate**.

Here's how to upgrade your spending awareness:

1. Know Your Spending Triggers

Are you most tempted late at night? After a hard day? During sales?

Awareness is your first line of defence.

2. Create a "Yes List"

Define in advance what you *do* want to spend on, quality food, occasional treats, experiences that matter.

Then say no to the rest without guilt.

3. Introduce Spending Rules

72-hour rule for non-essentials

1-in-1-out for clothes

Cash-only weeks to feel the money leaving your hand

4. Embrace the Power of "No"

Every time you say *no* to something you don't need, you say *yes* to something you really want, freedom, security, progress.

Key Insight: Avoiding Mistakes Builds Wealth Just as Fast as Making Money

People think wealth is built by adding more, more income, more investments, more hustle.

But often, the real breakthrough comes by *removing* the leaks.

You don't need to become a millionaire this year.
 But if you:

> Cancel £30/month in unused subscriptions

> Say no to £100/month in impulse buys

> Avoid £500/year in late fees or high-interest payments

You've just created a £1,500+ swing in your favour, *without earning a penny more.*

That's the kind of move that builds quiet wealth.

Real Story: Tariq's Turnaround Through Saying No

Tariq's shift didn't come from earning more. It came from *stopping the slow bleed*.

He took one evening, listed all his regular transactions, and made changes:

> Cancelled four subscriptions, £45/month saved

> Set a £50 monthly cap on takeaway and stuck to it

> Moved his card out of his Amazon account to reduce impulse buys

> Said no to three big social events and hosted a potluck instead

His friends noticed, but most respected him. A few even followed his lead.

By the end of the year:

> He'd cleared two credit cards

> Saved over £2,000

> Felt calmer, more confident, and in control

He didn't miss the stuff. He loved the *peace*.

Your Wealth-Building Action for This Chapter

Let's identify and plug your personal money traps.

Audit Your Subscriptions

Check all app stores, bank statements, and online accounts.

Cancel anything you haven't used in the last 30 days.

Create a "No List"

Write down 3–5 purchases or habits you'll say no to for the next 30 days.

Be specific: "Friday takeaway" or "late-night Amazon scrolls."

Unlink Your Card

From shopping apps, browsers, and buy-now-pay-later accounts.

Make purchases take longer and feel more real.

Set One Social Boundary

Choose a phrase to politely decline events or spending that don't align with your goals:

"That sounds great, but I'm on a savings mission right now, maybe next time."

✓ *Bonus:* Track how much you "don't spend" over the next 30 days. Redirect it to savings or debt.

Takeaway: What You Don't Spend Is as Powerful as What You Earn

Wealth isn't just about making the right moves.
It's also about avoiding the wrong ones.

Say no to impulse.
Say no to pressure.
Say no to anything that delays your progress.

And in doing so, say yes to a life that's truly yours, on your terms.

Because every pound you *don't* waste is a pound that builds your future.

Chapter 11: Making Small Investments Early

When Priya was 25, she started investing just **£50 a month** from her admin job salary. Her friends laughed when she mentioned it.
"What's the point? That's barely anything."

But Priya wasn't trying to get rich overnight. She just knew one thing:

> **The earlier you start, the less you need.**
> **The later you start, the more you'll pay.**

Twenty years later, still earning modestly, never contributing more than £100/month, Priya has over **£48,000** in her ISA and pension accounts, thanks to the magic of **compound interest**.

She didn't gamble. She didn't trade. She just invested early, consistently, and stayed the course.

Her story is a powerful reminder that **time is the real millionaire-maker**, not income.

Why Time Beats Amount in Investing

Let's talk about compound interest, the most powerful (and underused) force in personal finance.

Albert Einstein reportedly called it the eighth wonder of the world. Why? Because it's money that earns **more money**, without any extra effort from you.

Here's how it works:

> In Year 1, your £50/month investment grows to £600 + interest.

> In Year 2, you earn interest not just on your contributions, but on the interest you earned in Year 1.

> This repeats every year, snowballing your money faster and faster over time.

The earlier you start, the more powerful the effect. Even small amounts can grow dramatically if given enough years.

Example:

> £50/month invested over 20 years at 7% average annual return
> = **£25,000 contributed**
> = **~£48,000 total (including growth)**

Now compare that to someone who waits until their 40s and tries to "catch up" with £200/month. They may still fall short.

Start early. Start small. Let time do the heavy lifting.

How to Start Investing with £10–£50 a Month

Many people think investing is for the wealthy. But in 2025, it's easier than ever to start with almost nothing.

Here's a simple starter guide:

1. Choose a Platform

Use an investment app or provider that supports low minimums. Some good UK-based options:

> **Moneybox** (round-ups + £1–£10 starting options)

> **Nutmeg**, **Wealthify**, or **Plum**

> **Vanguard** (great for index funds, starting from £100 lump sum or £25/month)

2. Open the Right Account

Start with a **stocks and shares ISA**. It allows you to invest tax-free up to £20,000/year (don't worry, you don't need to hit that!).

Alternatively, if it's for retirement, consider:

Workplace pension (especially if your employer matches contributions)

SIPP (Self-Invested Personal Pension)

✓ *Pro tip:* Even if you just invest £25/month into your ISA, you're ahead of most people who never start.

3. Pick a Simple Investment: Index Funds

Forget stock picking. Forget trying to time the market.

The simplest, most effective way for beginners to invest is through **index funds**, which are baskets of hundreds or even thousands of companies.

When you buy one, you're instantly diversified.

Some popular ones:

FTSE 100 or FTSE All-Share (UK companies)

S&P 500 (Top US companies)

Global index funds (Vanguard LifeStrategy, Fidelity World Index)

They're:

Low cost (fees under 0.3%)

Broadly diversified

Consistently solid performers over time

You don't need to beat the market, you just need to be *in* the market.

---

4. Automate and Forget

Set up an automatic monthly contribution and leave it alone.

Don't try to time the dips. Don't panic during downturns. Just keep contributing.

That's how real wealth is built, *not by genius, but by consistency.*

Key Insight: Every Pound Invested Buys Future Freedom

Here's the truth that most people miss:

Every £10 invested now could become £20–£30 in the future.

Every month you invest is a month closer to freedom.

Investing isn't about getting rich quick, it's about buying back your time.

The longer your money works, the less *you* have to.

Priya, from earlier, may never earn six figures, but her investments are working 24/7. While she sleeps, her money grows. While she works, her wealth multiplies.

That's the real definition of financial independence.

Real Story: Priya's £50/Month to a Comfortable Future

Priya, an admin assistant from Leicester, began investing at 25 after attending a workplace financial wellness seminar. She had no finance background, but she took one piece of advice to heart: *"Start now. Even if it's small."*

She opened a stocks and shares ISA, chose a simple global index fund, and set up a £50/month direct debit. She never skipped a month.

Over time:

- She increased it to £75, then £100 as her salary grew
- She stayed invested through market drops, never pulling out
- She rarely checked her account, she trusted the process

At 45, she has:

- **£48,000+** in her ISA and pension combined
- **£12,000** in cash savings
- A plan to retire by 55, even on a modest income

Her friends, many of whom out-earn her, are now asking *her* for financial advice.

All because she made one quiet decision early, and stuck with it.

Your Wealth-Building Action for This Chapter

Let's get your first pound working for your future.

Open a Stocks and Shares ISA

Use an app or platform that feels user-friendly.

Set up your account this week.

Pick an Index Fund or Robo-Advisor Option

Choose a global or UK-focused low-cost index fund.

Don't obsess, just pick a broadly diversified option to start.

Set a Monthly Amount

£10, £25, or £50, whatever you can automate without stress.

Let It Run

Don't touch it. Don't panic. Review once every few months, *not every day.*

✅ *Bonus:* Use an investment calculator to see how much your current contribution could grow in 10, 20, or 30 years. Let the maths motivate you.

Takeaway: The Best Time to Invest Was Yesterday. The Second-Best Is Today.

You don't need a financial advisor, a six-figure salary, or a head for numbers.

You just need:

    A willingness to start

    A basic plan

    A bit of patience

Every pound you invest today is a future *you* buying back time, freedom, and peace.

So stop waiting.
Stop doubting.
Start small.
Start now.

Because time is on your side, *if* you let it work.

Chapter 12: Buying Assets, Not Liabilities

Darren had been saving for years. At 30, he had £12,000 tucked away, enough for something meaningful. His friends suggested the obvious:

> "Go on, mate, get yourself a new car. You've earned it."

And Darren was tempted. He liked the idea of pulling up in something sleek and shiny. The Audi A3 on finance looked good. Real good.

But instead, Darren used that £12,000 as a deposit on a small one-bedroom flat in Manchester, his first buy-to-let property. Modest. Not glamorous. But it earned him £250 a month in rental income from day one.

His friends had their dream cars.
Darren had an **income-generating asset**.

Five years later, he still drives a second-hand Ford Focus. But he now owns two rental properties and is on track to reach financial freedom before 45.

Why? Because Darren understood something most people miss:

> Some purchases make you feel rich.
> Others make you *actually* rich.

Assets vs Liabilities: The Defining Wealth Question

If you want to build real wealth, you need to master one distinction:

> **Does this thing put money *into* my pocket, or take money *out* of it?**

That's the difference between:

> **Assets** – things that generate income, grow in value, or increase your net worth.

> **Liabilities** – things that cost money, depreciate, or create long-term expenses.

Let's break it down.

Assets include:

> Investment properties

> Stocks and index funds

> Retirement accounts

> Businesses you own

Valuable skills or certifications that boost income

Tools or equipment that generate money

Liabilities include:

Cars (especially financed ones)

Expensive gadgets with no return

Designer clothes

Unused subscriptions

Anything that loses value and drains your cash

The key to wealth is simple:

> **Buy more assets. Avoid unnecessary liabilities.**

That doesn't mean you can't enjoy life. It means you enjoy it **intentionally**, and you prioritise purchases that build your future, not just your image.

Choosing Investments Over Consumption

Every time money hits your account, you're faced with a choice:

Spend it now on something that depreciates (new clothes, car upgrades, gadgets).

Invest it into something that appreciates (index fund, property, business, skill).

Let's say you get a £1,000 bonus.

Spend it on a weekend trip and it's gone (memories = great, but no financial return).

Spend it on shares of a global index fund, and it could grow to £2,000–£3,000+ over time.

This isn't about *never* spending money on fun.
It's about recognising that **some spending grows your freedom, and some delays it.**

Ask yourself:

"In five years, will this decision have helped me, or held me back?"

The Mindset Shift: From Spender to Asset-Builder

Building wealth isn't just about different habits. It's about a different identity.

Spenders say:

> "I deserve this now."

> "I'll start saving later."

> "I work hard, I should enjoy it."

Asset-builders say:

> "I want my money to work as hard as I do."

> "Every pound I keep is a soldier for my future."

> "I don't need to impress anyone, I'm building something real."

The shift is subtle, but powerful.

When you become an asset-builder:

> You ask better questions.

> You delay gratification *on purpose*.

You prioritise wealth-building decisions, not just income-earning ones.

And over time? You stop needing to hustle so hard, because your assets are doing the heavy lifting.

Real Story: Darren Chooses Property Over Prestige

Let's revisit Darren, the retail manager from Manchester.

He grew up modestly, no handouts, no financial education. But he developed an interest in money early and started saving £200/month at age 22.

By age 30, he'd saved £12,000. His plan? Buy his "dream car."

But after reading books like *Rich Dad Poor Dad* and listening to property investment podcasts, he changed course. Instead of spending it, he used the money as a deposit on a buy-to-let flat.

Here's what happened:

> He bought a £90,000 flat, with rental income of £600/month.

After costs, he cleared £250/month in passive profit.

He reinvested the profit and savings for another two years.

At 33, he bought a second flat.

At 35, his rental income covers over 50% of his monthly living expenses.

He still drives a used car.
He still lives modestly.
But he's *building a portfolio*, not a reputation.

That's what separates the flashy from the financially free.

Key Insight: Prioritise Things That Put Money in Your Pocket

Not all spending is equal.

There's spending that creates **temporary pleasure**, and spending that creates **long-term power**.

The goal is not to cut out joy. The goal is to buy **freedom before furniture**.
Assets before accessories. Security before status.

Because when your assets start paying your bills, everything changes:

You work because you *want* to, not because you have to.

You can handle emergencies without panic.

You sleep better at night, knowing your future is funded.

That's real wealth.

Your Wealth-Building Action for This Chapter

It's time to step into the asset-builder mindset.

List All the "Assets" and "Liabilities" You've Bought in the Last 12 Months

Be honest. Look at purchases over £100.

Categorise: Did this make you richer or poorer?

Choose One Asset to Prioritise Next

An index fund? A course or certification? A small savings pot for property? A side-hustle tool?

Pause One Liability Purchase

Delay a flashy or non-essential spend for 30 days.

Redirect that money into your chosen asset.

Create a Wealth Filter

Before any major purchase, ask:

"Will this grow my income, value, or future security?"

✅ *Bonus:* Rename your savings account to "Next Asset Fund." Let every pound in there remind you of the life you're building.

Takeaway: Flashy Spenders Impress Today, Asset Builders Win Tomorrow

You don't need to keep up with anyone.
You don't need the latest thing.
You need assets.

Things that:

    Grow your money

    Free up your time

    Build your legacy

Every pound you spend is a vote for the future you're building.

So choose assets.
Choose wisely.
Choose wealth.

Chapter 13: Using Windfalls Wisely

Laura stared at her payslip. A **£1,000 bonus**. Totally unexpected.

Her mind went wild:
A new sofa? A weekend away? A full wardrobe refresh?

But she paused.

Laura had been reading about wealth-building, about compound interest, assets, and long-term thinking. And for the first time, she didn't just want to *spend* the money. She wanted to *multiply* it.

She did something bold.

She took £700 and put it into a global index fund. She used £200 to pay off a lingering credit card balance. And she treated herself to a £100 spa day.

Three years later, her investments have grown. Her debt is gone. And she credits that bonus with being the moment her **financial journey truly began**.

The lesson?

> Windfalls don't change your life, what you *do* with them does.

What Counts as a Windfall?

You might think windfalls are just winning the lottery or receiving a massive inheritance.

But in reality, windfalls happen all the time:

- A **tax refund**
- An **annual bonus** at work
- A **gift** from family
- A **side hustle payout**
- A **refund** from overpaid bills
- A **rebate** or claim settlement

The problem?

Most people spend windfalls like found money.
Easy come, easy go. No plan. No pause.

But every windfall is a golden opportunity to **accelerate your wealth journey, if you're intentional.**

Why Most People Blow It (and How to Avoid It)

Here's what usually happens:

A lump sum appears.

The brain shouts: *"We're rich!"*

Spending begins, big treat, upgrade, or splurge.

A week later, it's gone. Nothing's changed.

The cycle repeats.

This is called **"blow it syndrome."** And it's rooted in a scarcity mindset, thinking this money is rare and must be enjoyed *now* before it vanishes.

But what if you approached windfalls with an **abundance mindset**?

Instead of seeing the money as a short-term high, you treat it like a seed, something that, if planted properly, can grow into *much more*.

The Golden Rule of Windfalls: Split, Don't Spend

When a lump sum shows up, don't blow it, **break it up.**

Here's a smart formula to apply:

✅ The 50–30–20 Rule for Windfalls

50% to your future (investing, savings, debt repayment)

30% to your present (immediate needs or goals)

20% to enjoy (guilt-free fun, spending, experience)

Example: £1,000 Bonus

£500 into index fund or emergency fund

£300 to fix your car, buy tools, or take a course

£200 for a weekend trip or something fun

This approach balances progress with joy. You feel the reward, but you also *build with it.*

The trick? **Decide in advance.** Before the money even lands, make a plan. Remove emotion. Act with clarity.

3 Common Windfalls, And What to Do With Them

1. Tax Refunds

Often seen as free money. But really, it's just *your* money coming back to you.

Smart play:

- Pay off high-interest debt first

- Top up your emergency fund

- Invest into a stocks and shares ISA

- Save a small % for a treat to avoid burnout

2. Work Bonuses

Bonuses are income, not a shopping spree.

Smart play:

- Use part to upgrade your skills or tools that make you more valuable

- Put a chunk toward long-term investments

Revisit your financial goals, what could this bonus unlock?

3. Inheritance or Gifts

This one can be emotional. But even small inheritances (£500–£5,000) can make a big impact when used wisely.

Smart play:

Create a "legacy plan", how will this money honour the person who gave it?

Avoid making huge decisions immediately, pause, reflect, then act

Use part to secure your future: property deposit, debt clearance, or investment

---

Key Insight: Windfalls Accelerate Wealth When Handled Intentionally

You don't need to win the lottery.
You just need to *stop wasting the lucky breaks you already get*.

A £500 side hustle payout could:

Pay off a credit card

Buy a course that unlocks £1,000 in future income

Grow into £1,000+ in an index fund over time

The magic isn't in the amount.
It's in the *mindset*. The *decision*. The *plan*.

Because without a plan, money finds a way to disappear.
 But with a plan? Even modest windfalls can **catapult your progress.**

Real Story: Laura's £1,000 Bonus That Changed Everything

Laura worked in customer service. Her annual bonus varied, but one year, to her surprise, she got £1,000.

Past Laura would've bought a new phone or booked a flight.

But something had shifted.

She split the bonus using her own version of the 50–30–20 rule:

£700 into a Vanguard index fund

£200 to finally clear an annoying credit card balance

£100 to treat herself to a massage and a nice dinner

It didn't feel restrictive. It felt empowering.

That investment? It's now worth more than £1,200.
The credit card? Still at zero.
The treat? Still memorable, but not followed by guilt.

She credits that one windfall as the *turning point* in her relationship with money.

Your Wealth-Building Action for This Chapter

Plan ahead for your next windfall, before it arrives.

Create a Windfall Strategy

> Decide in advance how you'll divide any unexpected money.
>
> Write it down. Use 50–30–20 or your own formula.

Reflect on Past Windfalls

What did you do with your last tax refund, bonus, or gift?

What would you do differently now?

Visualise the Impact

Use a compound interest calculator to see how a one-off investment could grow.

Remind yourself: *Every lump sum is a lever.*

Start a "Windfall Wins" Jar

Each time you use a windfall wisely, track the progress.

Celebrate your discipline and future-focused thinking.

✓ *Bonus Tip:* If you struggle with spending discipline, automate windfall splits, have 50% routed straight to savings/investment the moment it hits.

Takeaway: Windfalls Won't Build Wealth, *You* Will

A windfall is a spark.
But you're the firestarter.

Used recklessly, it's gone in days.
Used wisely, it becomes a **catalyst for financial change**.

So when the next bonus, refund, or unexpected cheque comes your way, pause. Breathe. Plan.

And make it count.

Because wealth isn't built on luck. It's built on *what you do* with it.

Chapter 14: Teaching Wealth Principles to Family

When Malcolm handed his 17-year-old daughter, Aisha, a debit card tied to her own student savings account, he didn't say much, just:

> "This is your money. You decide what to do with it. But remember: every pound has a job."

He'd been dropping little lessons like that for years. No lectures. No guilt trips. Just consistent nudges.

By the time Aisha turned 18, she had:

> Her first part-time job
>
> A cash emergency fund
>
> Zero debt
>
> A basic understanding of saving, investing, and conscious spending

While her classmates were opening student overdrafts and racking up credit cards, Aisha was planning to graduate with **no debt and a growing investment account.**

Malcolm didn't just build wealth for himself, he passed it on. Quietly. Deliberately. And that, perhaps, is the most powerful kind of wealth building there is.

Real wealth isn't just what you accumulate. It's what you pass on.

Breaking Generational Money Patterns

Many of us grew up in households where money was:

Not talked about

Feared

Fought over

Or used as a tool of control

We may have inherited unhelpful beliefs like:

"We're just not good with money."

"Money doesn't grow on trees."

"Rich people are selfish."

"Debt is normal."

These generational patterns often shape how we earn, spend, save, and think about money, even without realising it.

But here's the truth:

You can be the turning point.

You don't need a finance degree or perfect habits.
You just need **awareness**, a **willingness to learn**, and the **courage to talk about money differently** with the people you love.

Simple Ways to Raise Financially Savvy Kids (or Influence Family)

You don't need to preach to be a teacher. You just need to model better habits and open up the conversation.

Here are a few simple, everyday ways to teach wealth-building at home:

✅ 1. Talk About Money Openly (and Age-Appropriately)

Don't wait until kids are in crisis to introduce financial concepts. Start early:

With young children: explain where money comes from, and the idea of exchanging it for goods.

With teens: show them how a budget works, what things cost, and how savings grow.

With adult family: share what you're learning, what's working, and offer tools (not lectures).

Pro tip: Don't make money a taboo subject. Make it a normal one.

✅ 2. Let Them Manage Small Sums Themselves

Give kids some money they control. Not endless handouts, just structured independence:

- A small allowance with clear boundaries

- A prepaid debit card (like GoHenry or Starling Kite)

- A rule: once it's gone, it's gone

They'll learn quickly, and safely, through experience.

✅ 3. Share Your Wealth Journey (Mistakes and All)

One of the most powerful things you can do is be honest about your own wins and losses:

> "I wish I'd started saving earlier."

> "Here's how I cleared my debt."

> "This is what I'm investing in, and why."

You're not lecturing, you're storytelling. And storytelling sticks.

✅ 4. Gamify Financial Learning

Learning about money doesn't have to be dry.

- Use games like Monopoly, Cashflow, or budgeting apps to teach.

- Challenge your kids to save for something instead of just buying it.

- Do "spending-free weekends" as a family adventure.

✅ **5. Celebrate Smart Money Choices**

When a child saves, budgets, or thinks long-term, acknowledge it.

> "That was a really smart way to compare prices."

> "You saved up for that? Impressive!"

> "You said no to something you didn't really need. That's maturity."

Encouragement builds confidence. Confidence builds behaviour.

How to Influence Family Without Preaching

You might not be raising kids, but you might still want to influence your partner, siblings, or even parents.

This can be tricky. Money is personal. Defensive. Emotional.

Here's how to do it without alienating anyone:

➤ **Start With "What I'm Learning," Not "What You Should Do"**

People hate being told they're wrong. But they're curious about what works.

Say:

"I started tracking my spending, and it's helping."

"This podcast changed how I think about debt."

"I read something cool about investing £50/month, I didn't realise how powerful that could be."

You're not correcting them. You're inviting them to explore.

➤ Lead With Questions, Not Judgements

Instead of: "You spend too much on takeaways,"
Try: "Do you ever think about where most of your money goes?"

Let them discover. Don't dictate.

➤ Be the Example

Consistency beats conversation. When people see you:

Avoiding debt

Saving regularly

Staying calm in financial situations

Investing with confidence

They'll ask how. That's your moment.

Key Insight: Teaching Multiplies Wealth Across Generations

You're not just building wealth for you. You're modelling a new standard for everyone around you.

When a child sees:

Money being talked about calmly

Savings treated as normal

Investing as something ordinary people do

They grow up thinking it's *expected*, not *exceptional*.

You don't just create wealth, you create a **legacy mindset**.

That ripples out in ways you'll never fully see, but will absolutely be felt.

Real Story: Malcolm Raises a Money-Smart Teen

Malcolm was a single dad working as a delivery driver. He didn't grow up with wealth, but he was determined to raise his daughter differently.

He started small:

- Gave Aisha a basic allowance at age 10
- Talked openly about bills and budgeting
- Used shopping trips as lessons in value vs cost
- Let her save for her first smartphone instead of buying it for her

At 16, Aisha opened her first junior ISA. By 17, she had a part-time job and a savings tracker.

At 18, while others were preparing for university debt, Aisha had already built a £2,000 emergency fund.

She plans to study finance, and credits her dad not for preaching, but for *practising* what he wanted her to learn.

Your Wealth-Building Action for This Chapter

Time to become the mentor your family needs, gently, intentionally, and powerfully.

Start One Money Conversation This Week

With a child, partner, sibling, or friend.

Share a story, ask a question, or explain one habit that's helped you.

Set Up One Simple Teaching Moment

Let a child manage a small budget.

Involve your teen in the weekly food shop planning.

Show a family member how you track expenses.

Reflect on What You Learned About Money

What did your parents teach (or not teach)?

What do you want to pass on, or break free from?

Choose One Resource to Share

A book, video, app, or podcast.

Not as a correction, but as an "I thought of you" gift.

✓ *Bonus:* Create a simple "Family Wealth Values" list. One page. Just the basics:

Save before spending

Avoid debt

Invest early

Learn continuously

Help others grow too

Takeaway: You're Not Just Building Wealth, You're Building Legacy

Money lessons echo for generations.
And the best time to plant them is now.

So be the conversation starter.
Be the model.
Be the reason someone in your family never fears money again.

Because teaching wealth isn't just kind, it's **transformational**.

Chapter 15: Building Wealth with Community Support

When Imran joined a money challenge group on Facebook, he wasn't expecting much. Just a few people tracking savings goals. Maybe the occasional budgeting tip.

But after three months of being part of that community, something had shifted:

> He was saving consistently.

> He'd paid off a lingering credit card.

> He was reading books on investing, for the first time in his life.

What changed?

> It wasn't a raise. It wasn't luck. It was **accountability**.
> It was **community**.

He wasn't building wealth alone anymore, and that made all the difference.

The Myth of the Lone Wealth Builder

There's a romanticised idea in personal finance: the lone wolf hustling in silence, grinding their way to riches. No support. No help. Just grit.

But in reality? That's not how most successful people build wealth.

Behind most financially empowered individuals is:

A supportive **partner**, friend, or mentor

A community of like-minded individuals

A consistent dose of accountability

Why?

Because let's be honest: this stuff is hard to stick with in isolation.

You get tired.
You second-guess yourself.
You hit plateaus.
You're surrounded by a world telling you to spend, upgrade, indulge.

That's where **community** comes in.

Why Accountability Increases Success

Studies show that people are:

65% more likely to meet a goal when they commit to someone else.

95% more likely when they have a scheduled check-in.

That's not weakness. That's human psychology.

Accountability helps because it:

Reminds you of your goals when motivation dips.

Reduces isolation, you're not the only one being frugal or investing.

Celebrates small wins that would otherwise go unnoticed.

Offers real solutions when you feel stuck.

In short:

You go further when you go together.

How to Find a Wealth-Building Community

You don't need to wait for one to appear. Start by choosing your level of involvement.

✓ 1. Join Online Personal Finance Communities

There are thriving groups out there for every niche:

- UK-based savings groups (e.g. "Frugal & Thriving UK" on Facebook)
- FIRE (Financial Independence, Retire Early) forums
- Reddit threads like r/UKPersonalFinance
- Discord servers or WhatsApp groups focused on budgeting

Start by observing. Then engage. Ask questions. Share goals. Learn out loud.

✓ 2. Attend Money Workshops, Webinars, or Local Meetups

Look for:

- Library-hosted budgeting workshops

Online webinars from trusted financial educators

University adult education courses

Church or community group classes

In-person or not, the key is consistency, *show up regularly.*

✓ 3. Start a Mini Mastermind or Accountability Group

Don't overcomplicate it. Just invite:

One friend who wants to get out of debt

A sibling who's saving for a house

A colleague who's interested in investing

Agree to meet or check in monthly:

Share a win, a challenge, and a next step.

Keep each other on track, without shame.

Even a **duo** can be a game-changer.

✅ **4. Follow Mentors Who Share Your Values**

You don't need to know them personally. Follow financial role models who:

- Talk in terms that make sense

- Share real-life strategies

- Align with your goals (especially those on modest incomes)

Some mentors you may never meet. But their voice can keep you going.

Avoiding Environments That Normalise Overspending

As much as support helps, **sabotage is real too.**

Watch out for:

- Friends who joke about being "bad with money" like it's a badge of honour

Family who pressure you to spend to prove love

Workplaces with toxic "spend to fit in" cultures

You don't have to cut people off. But you **can** create boundaries.

Say:

"That's not in my plan right now."

"I'm working on a goal, let's find a cheaper option."

"I've got a budget for this month, so I'll pass."

You're not judging. You're leading by example.

And soon enough? You'll start attracting others who want the same.

Real Story: Imran Finds Strength in Community

Imran was a 28-year-old admin assistant in Leeds. Decent salary, but always felt like he had "nothing to show for it." Savings? Zero. Debt? Growing. Motivation? Missing.

Then one night, scrolling Instagram, he came across a post:
"Join our 90-Day £1,000 Savings Challenge!"

He clicked. It was free. Low pressure. Just a Facebook group of people committed to saving small, consistent amounts. Daily tips. Weekly check-ins. Celebration posts.

So he joined.

Here's what changed:

He created a simple savings tracker.

He posted his goal and progress weekly.

He watched others win, and felt inspired, not jealous.

He saved £1,050 in 3 months. More than he'd ever saved before.

But the biggest win?
He stopped feeling ashamed about money, and started feeling **empowered**.

He stayed in the group. Started offering encouragement to others. Became a leader. And now? He's planning to help others run their own savings challenges.

All from one decision: *"I don't want to do this alone anymore."*

Key Insight: Community Keeps You Going When Motivation Dips

Willpower fades.
Life gets busy.
Old habits creep in.

But **community reminds you of who you're becoming.**

You start thinking:

"I can do this."

"They're doing it, too."

"I'm not weird for caring about money, I'm smart."

Community gives your goals **roots and wings**.

Your Wealth-Building Action for This Chapter

Join One Money-Minded Group This Week

Facebook, Reddit, Discord, or local. Doesn't matter, just start.

Engage once. Comment. Ask. Learn. Share.

Create a Check-In System

Text a friend weekly about your financial win and challenge.

Set a monthly "Wealth Check" reminder for yourself.

Audit Your Environment

Who in your life makes wealth-building easier?

Who normalises habits you want to break?

Where can you spend more time to level up?

Be the Invitation

Invite one person into your journey.

Share a podcast, book, or goal.

Start the money conversation others are waiting for.

✓ *Bonus Tip:* If your current circle doesn't get it, build a new one. One person at a time.

Takeaway: Wealth-Building Is Personal, But It Doesn't Have to Be Lonely

You don't need to do this alone.
You weren't meant to.

There are people out there saving, investing, learning, *just like you*.
Find them. Lean on them. Be one of them.

Because when you surround yourself with people who believe in wealth, even on a modest income, you stop feeling behind.

You start feeling **powerful**.

Chapter 16: Protecting Your Progress

When Priya was diagnosed with breast cancer at 36, the shock rippled through every part of her life. As a freelance designer, her income stopped almost immediately.

But what didn't stop?

Her mortgage repayments.
Her energy bills.
Her need for food, transport, and care.

What saved her wasn't luck, it was **preparation**.

Years earlier, she'd taken out a modest **critical illness policy**. She had a fully funded **emergency fund**, and she'd arranged **income protection insurance**.

The result?

>She could focus on treatment, not bills.

>She didn't go into debt.

>Her financial goals weren't destroyed.

In her words:

"I didn't realise how powerful my boring financial decisions were, until they saved my future."

Why Protection Is the Missing Piece in Wealth Conversations

We often talk about:

Saving

Budgeting

Investing

Earning more

But rarely do we talk about *protecting* what we're building.

Yet what's the point of all your hard work, if one accident, illness, or disaster can wipe it out?

Wealth isn't just about growth.
It's also about **resilience**.

This chapter is your blueprint for **locking in your financial progress**, so your future isn't left vulnerable to chance.

The Most Common Threats to Wealth

Let's talk about what can derail even the best money plans:

Job loss

Illness or injury

Unexpected expenses

Family emergencies

Death of a provider

Legal issues or accidents

These aren't hypothetical, they're **inevitable** at some point in life. And if you're unprotected, they can cause:

Debt spirals

Lost homes

Ruined savings

Years of financial setback

That's why the smart move isn't to live in fear, it's to **plan ahead**.

The Three Layers of Financial Protection

Let's break it down into three critical safety nets.

✅ 1. Emergency Fund – Your First Line of Defence

This is your self-insurance, the buffer between you and chaos.

What it is:
A pot of savings set aside for true emergencies only (not holidays or new sofas).

Ideal amount:

- 3–6 months of living expenses
- Minimum £1,000 starter emergency fund if you're just beginning

Use it for:

- Job loss

Medical costs

Car repairs

Urgent home fixes

Top tip:
Keep it in a separate easy-access savings account, not your current account. Out of sight, out of temptation.

✅ 2. Insurance – The Safety Net You Hope You Never Need

a. Income Protection Insurance
If you're unable to work due to illness or injury, this covers a % of your income (often 50–70%).

Why it matters:
Especially crucial for self-employed or freelance workers.

b. Critical Illness Cover
Pays a lump sum if diagnosed with a serious illness (like cancer, heart attack, stroke).

Why it matters:
Gives breathing room to recover without financial ruin.

c. Life Insurance
Pays a sum to your dependents if you pass away.

Why it matters:
Ensures your loved ones aren't financially stranded.

Note: These don't have to cost a fortune. Even £10–£30/month can give powerful peace of mind. The key is **choosing a level that fits your needs and budget.**

✅ **3. Wills and Legal Protection – The Future Guardrails**

Wills aren't just for the rich.

If you have:

- Children
- Property
- Savings
- Any wishes for your money after death

Then you need a will.

It ensures:

- Your assets go where *you* choose

- Your children have guardians

- You avoid costly legal disputes for your family

You can make one affordably online (or with a solicitor for more complex cases).

Lasting Power of Attorney (LPA):
Let's someone you trust make decisions for you if you become incapacitated.

It's a gift of control, to your future self.

Proactive Steps That Prevent Wealth Erosion

Building wealth is only half the game. The other half is **keeping it safe**.

Here's your protective action plan:

✅ Step 1: Build or Review Your Emergency Fund

Start with £500–£1,000

- Build toward 3–6 months of core living costs

- Automate a small amount weekly if needed (£10–£20 adds up)

✅ Step 2: Get the Right Insurances

- Start with life insurance if you have dependents

- Add critical illness cover or income protection if self-employed

- Use comparison tools like MoneySuperMarket or CompareTheMarket to get quotes

✅ Step 3: Write or Update Your Will

- Use a solicitor or reputable online service (like Farewill or Co-op Legal Services)

- Update every few years, or after major life events (marriage, children, property)

✅ Step 4: Secure a Power of Attorney (Optional but Wise)

Especially important if you're single, ageing, or want extra safeguards

Protects your finances and health decisions if you're ever unable to decide for yourself

---

Real Story: Priya's Protection Plan Saved Her

Priya had always been sensible with money. Nothing fancy, just steady habits.

But it was a chance encounter at a financial wellbeing workshop that prompted her to:

Take out a £30/month critical illness policy

Build a three-month emergency fund

Get income protection as a freelancer

Two years later, when her diagnosis came, she said it was like the old her had sent the future her a gift.

The insurance paid out £40,000. She didn't need to touch her investments. She didn't sell her home. She didn't spiral into debt.

Instead, she recovered in peace, returned to part-time work, and is now mentoring others on financial resilience.

Her takeaway?

> "You don't build a safety net because you expect to fall. You build it so you can *bounce back* when you do."

Key Insight: Building Wealth Is Pointless If It's Vulnerable to Disaster

You can do everything right, save, budget, invest, and still be derailed by one crisis… **unless you've prepared.**

Protection might not feel exciting.
It doesn't sparkle like a new investment portfolio.
But it's the **silent strength** behind lasting wealth.

And the best part?
You can build it gradually.
You can build it affordably.
And you can start today.

Your Wealth-Building Action for This Chapter

Audit Your Financial Protection

Do you have an emergency fund?

What insurances do you have (or need)?

Do you have a will?

Pick One Area to Strengthen This Week

Open a savings account for emergencies

Get a life insurance quote

Book an appointment to create a will

Talk to Someone You Trust

Let your partner or family know your protection plan

Review each other's gaps together

✓ *Bonus Tip:* Set a calendar reminder to review your protections annually, especially after big life changes.

Takeaway: True Wealth Isn't Just What You Accumulate, It's What You Can Protect

You've worked hard to get here.
Now it's time to **lock it in**.

Because real freedom doesn't just come from what you earn.
It comes from knowing you, and your family, are safe.

So do the "boring" things now.
Your future self will thank you.

Chapter 17: Multiplying Wealth Over Time

When Martina first started budgeting, she was a 23-year-old receptionist earning £19,000 a year. No savings. No plan. Just a vague sense that money kept slipping through her fingers.

By 33, she had:

> A fully funded emergency fund
>
> £45,000 in a low-cost investment portfolio
>
> A small rental property worth £110,000 with £30,000 equity
>
> And zero debt

Her net worth had passed £100,000.

She didn't win the lottery. She didn't get a windfall. She didn't even get massive promotions.

She simply followed the same modest, consistent practices, for **ten straight years**.

> Slow. Steady. Repeatable.
> That's the quiet power of multiplying wealth over time.

The Myth of "Getting Rich Quick"

We live in a world obsessed with overnight success:

"How I turned £500 into £50,000 with crypto!"

"Why you need 7 income streams to get rich by 30"

"10x your income this year!"

But behind most real, lasting wealth is something much less glamorous, and far more powerful:

Consistency over time.

It's not flashy. It's not sexy. But it works.

And in this chapter, we'll talk about how to **multiply your wealth sustainably**, without burning out, gambling, or losing sight of what really matters.

Adding Income Streams as Confidence Grows

Let's be clear: **multiple income streams aren't required to get wealthy.**

But they are an excellent strategy for:

Building faster

Creating financial safety

Increasing options

The key? You don't need *seven* streams. You need *one at a time*, done well.

✅ Start with What You Know

You don't need to reinvent yourself. Look at:

Skills you already use in your day job (teaching, admin, writing, coaching)

Hobbies you enjoy (crafts, gaming, gardening, fitness)

Problems you've solved for yourself (budgeting, home organisation, meal prepping)

Could you turn any of those into:

A freelance service

An online course

A paid consultation

A weekend side gig?

✅ Keep It Low-Risk and Part-Time

You don't need to quit your job. Start small:

1–2 hours per week

No major upfront costs

Learn as you go

The confidence you gain from one small win is fuel to take the next step.

Scaling Savings and Investments as Income Increases

When your income rises, so should your savings and investing.

But here's the trap: **lifestyle inflation.**

It whispers:

> "You've earned this. Go upgrade."

> "You can afford to spend more now."

> "Treat yourself."

And while there's nothing wrong with enjoying your income, here's the better move:

> Every time your income goes up, *increase your savings rate first.*

Let's say you get a £200/month raise:

- Put £100 into investments
- Use £50 to pay off debt or boost savings
- Enjoy £50 guilt-free

Do that consistently and:

- Your wealth snowballs
- Your lifestyle stays under control
- Your financial freedom accelerates

✅ **The Rule of Halves (Optional Strategy)**

Every time your income increases:

Save/invest 50%

Use 50% for enjoyment or flexibility

That way, you *enjoy the present*, without robbing your future.

Staying Humble as Wealth Builds

There's a sneaky danger when things start going well: **complacency** or **ego**.

You hit £10k in savings, then coast.
You buy a rental and feel like a property mogul.
You start judging others for "not getting it."

That's when financial growth stalls, or reverses.

Here's how to stay grounded:

➤ **Stay a Student**

Keep learning. Read books. Listen to podcasts. Stay curious.

➤ **Reflect on the Journey**

Look back every six months and remind yourself how far you've come, and how much more there is to build.

➤ **Don't Compete, Inspire**

You're not here to "win" at wealth. You're here to create freedom, and invite others along.

True wealth builds humility, not ego.

Key Insight: Slow, Steady Scaling Wins

The most common story in wealth-building isn't:

"I made a million overnight."

It's:

"I kept showing up."

Wealth multiplies when you:

Stick to your system

Improve your percentage slowly

Celebrate progress over perfection

Because when you keep doing the right things, even at a small scale, they compound.

And compounding is what **quietly turns effort into freedom.**

Real Story: Martina's 10-Year Journey to £100k

Martina didn't have a grand plan. But she had a commitment:

"I don't want to feel broke anymore."

So she made a budget. Opened a LISA (Lifetime ISA). Started investing £50/month into an index fund. Took on the occasional weekend catering gig. Said no to upgrading her car, even when she could. Learned from podcasts. Took notes. Stayed the course.

Some years were harder than others. But she never stopped.

By age 33, her net worth was just over £100,000. No drama. No headline. Just quiet, consistent wealth-building.

Her friends asked how she did it. Her answer?

"I kept it boring, and I kept going."

Your Wealth-Building Action for This Chapter

Let's set the stage for your next level of financial growth.

Review Your Income Streams

How many do you have?

Are they active or passive?

Which ones can you improve or expand?

Commit to Scaling One Area

Increase your monthly investing amount by £10–£50

Save a portion of any raise or windfall

Start a low-risk side gig

Set a 1-Year Wealth Milestone

"I want to reach £X net worth by next August."

"I want to increase my savings rate to 25%."

"I want to add one new income stream."

Schedule a Wealth Review

Every quarter, review:

Your net worth

Your income/savings progress

What you learned

What's next

✓ *Bonus Tip:* Write a letter to your future self at your next wealth milestone. Describe what you're doing now, and what you hope they've achieved.

Takeaway: Wealth Grows When You Do, Gradually, Intentionally, Quietly

You don't need fireworks.
You don't need overnight success.
You just need patience, persistence, and a plan.

Because the truth is:

> You're already capable of building £100k, £500k, or more.

You just need to keep stacking small wins, over and over again.

Chapter 18: Avoiding Sabotage as Income Grows

It started with a raise.

Then came the upgraded phone.

Then the new car on finance.

Then the rented flat with a "nicer postcode" and the weekly dinner deliveries.

By the time Olivia sat down to check her bank account six months later, her income had increased by £600 a month, but her savings had decreased, her credit card balance had ballooned, and her stress levels had never been higher.

> More money.
> Worse results.
> How?

She hadn't developed worse habits.
 She just didn't update the systems that helped her grow in the first place.

The Income Illusion: "I Make More, So I'm Fine"

There's a dangerous assumption that comes with earning more:

> "Now that I make more, I don't need to worry as much."

You stop budgeting.
You skip savings contributions "just this month."
You justify bigger purchases, after all, you can afford them now.

But here's the truth:

> **If you don't master money at £2,000/month, you won't suddenly master it at £4,000/month.**

More income gives you *more room for error*.
It doesn't automatically give you *more wisdom*.

That only comes from awareness, discipline, and intentionality.

The Sneaky Cost of Lifestyle Creep

Lifestyle creep happens when your spending quietly expands to match your increased income.

It sounds like:

"We deserve a nicer car now."

"Let's move somewhere with more space, even if it's pricier."

"What's the point of earning more if we don't enjoy it?"

Enjoyment isn't the problem. It's **automatic spending** without checking whether it serves your values or long-term goals.

Let's compare two paths:

Scenario A – Lifestyle Creep:

Income increases £500/month

All of it goes to new subscriptions, upgrades, eating out, impulse spending

Wealth stays flat

Scenario B – Intentional Scaling:

Income increases £500/month

£250/month goes to investments

£150/month to fun money

£100/month into a holiday fund

Same raise.
Radically different outcomes.

Why Wealth Builders Stay Humble with More Income

Wealthy people don't stay wealthy because they earn more.
They stay wealthy because they **manage more with the same mindset that got them started**.

That means:

- Continuing to budget, even when it's easy not to

- Increasing savings and investments as income rises

- Checking in with financial goals regularly

- Living *slightly* below their means, even when their means grow

The more money you have, the more **leverage**, but also the more **responsibility**.

Just like lifting heavier weights requires better form, **handling more money requires stronger systems**.

How to Reaffirm Goals and Systems at Every Level

The goal is never perfection, it's **upgrading your financial operating system** as your life changes.

Here's how to do it:

✅ 1. Revisit Your Financial Vision Every 6 Months

Ask:

> What does financial freedom still mean to me?
>
> Have my values shifted?
>
> Am I still on track, or just coasting?

Put it in writing. Read it monthly.

✅ 2. Recalculate Your Ideal Spending Plan

Are you still spending according to what matters?

Are you overspending in categories "just because you can"?

Can you save more now, without sacrificing joy?

✓ 3. Build Guardrails for New Income

Set rules:

"50% of any raise goes to long-term wealth."

"Any windfall is split: 40% invest, 30% save, 20% enjoy, 10% give."

"I won't upgrade my lifestyle unless I hit my next financial milestone."

Systems beat willpower. Set the system once, then stick to it.

✓ 4. Regularly Audit Habits That Creep In

Every 3 months:

Review subscriptions

Check card statements for "leaks"

Ask: "Would I still spend this if I earned half as much?"

Real Story: Olivia's Wake-Up Call

Olivia had worked hard to get promoted from junior administrator to marketing executive. Her salary jumped from £24,000 to £31,000. Suddenly, she felt like she'd "made it."

She moved into a newer flat, leased a car she'd been eyeing, and stopped checking her budget. She deserved this, didn't she?

Six months later:

Credit card balance: £3,200

Emergency fund: gone

Stress: through the roof

Her turning point came when she sat down with a friend who had never earned more than £27,000 but had over £12,000 in savings and was investing monthly.

Shocked, Olivia re-examined her habits. She:

- Downgraded to a smaller flat
- Sold the leased car and used public transport
- Created a "50/30/20" budget
- Committed to saving 25% of her income

Within a year, she was back in control, and more financially confident than ever.

Her lesson?

> "Money didn't change me. It just revealed the habits I stopped paying attention to."

Key Insight: Bigger Income = Bigger Responsibility

It's easy to think your income is the solution to your money problems. But the real solution is **how you handle it**.

With every extra pound comes a choice:

Expand your wealth, or your lifestyle.

Grow your freedom, or your obligations.

Cement your progress, or sabotage it.

When you treat a bigger income as a bigger opportunity to live on purpose, wealth follows.

Your Wealth-Building Action for This Chapter

Review the Last Time Your Income Increased

What did you do with the extra money?

Did your habits improve or decline?

What would you change if you could do it again?

Reaffirm Your Current Financial Goals

Write them down.

Make them visible.

Connect each one to a real emotional driver (peace, freedom, choice).

Set a Rule for Future Raises

Decide now how you'll handle the next raise, bonus, or side income.

Examples:

Save 50%, spend 30%, give 20%

Invest any new income above your current lifestyle

Perform a Financial Spring Clean

Cancel one subscription

Set a calendar reminder to review goals monthly

Commit to a no-spend week or challenge this month

✓ *Bonus Tip:* Share your rules with someone you trust. Accountability makes them stick.

Takeaway: The Goal Isn't Just to Earn More, It's to Handle More with Wisdom

More income isn't your golden ticket.

It's your next test.

And when you handle it with clarity, purpose, and upgraded systems, that test becomes your **launchpad**.

You don't just grow richer, you grow stronger.

Chapter 19: Redefining Wealth as Freedom

What does it mean to be wealthy?

Is it a number in a bank account?
A luxury car in the driveway?
A postcode that makes people nod approvingly?

Or is it something quieter, less flashy, more powerful?

For Lewis, real wealth wasn't about becoming rich. It was about no longer dreading Mondays.

He worked in a high-pressure sales job for years, £60,000 salary, company car, performance bonuses. To the outside world, he was doing well.

But inside? He was drained. Unfulfilled. Burnt out.

At age 38, after quietly saving and investing for nearly a decade, he finally did something extraordinary:

He quit, with a plan.

He took a part-time role at a local charity, began freelance consulting on the side, and for the first time in years, he had time to breathe. Time to think. Time to live.

"It wasn't about quitting work. It was about reclaiming my life," Lewis said.
"Wealth gave me options."

Why True Wealth Isn't About Status or Things

So many of us chase wealth for what we think it will give us:

Admiration

Success

Significance

Comfort

But when we dig deeper, what we really want isn't status, it's **freedom**.

Freedom to:

Choose how we spend our time

Walk away from toxic environments

Be present with our kids

Say "no" to what drains us and "yes" to what lights us up

Here's the twist:

You don't need a million pounds to feel wealthy.
You need control over your time, energy, and choices.

Linking Financial Goals to Time Freedom, Peace, and Purpose

Let's get real, money itself isn't meaningful. It's just a tool.

The power of money comes from how you **use** it.

So rather than setting vague goals like "I want to be rich" or "I want to earn more," ask yourself:

What kind of life do I want to live?

How do I want to spend my time?

What do I want to say "no" to?

What would peace look like in my everyday routine?

Then, link your financial goals to those answers.

Example:

Goal: Build a £20,000 buffer
Why: So I can leave a draining job and take 6 months to find meaningful work

Goal: Invest £300/month
Why: To retire early and travel with my partner in our 50s

Goal: Save £5,000 emergency fund
Why: So I can breathe, sleep better, and stop worrying about car repairs or surprise bills

When your goals are tied to your **freedom**, they become emotionally charged, and easier to stick to.

Avoiding the Trap of Endlessly Chasing "More"

Let's talk about the never-ending hamster wheel:

You get a raise… then want a bigger house

You buy a car... then feel it's not as nice as your friend's

You save £10k... but now you want £20k before you feel safe

The finish line keeps moving. Satisfaction always seems one step ahead.

This is called the **"more" trap**. And it's everywhere.

But here's the truth:

If you're always chasing more, you'll never feel like you have enough, even when you do.

That's why redefining wealth as **freedom and contentment** is the ultimate reset.

It doesn't mean you stop growing. It means you grow with purpose, not pressure.

Key Insight: Wealth Is Measured in Choices, Not Numbers

Here's what real wealth looks like:

Being able to say "no" to a job you hate

Being home for dinner with your family every night

Taking a walk at 2pm on a weekday because your time is yours

Sleeping peacefully, knowing you're not one emergency away from disaster

These are the things no luxury item can replace.

Because the richest people aren't always the ones with the biggest incomes.
 They're the ones with the most **control over their lives**.

Real Story: Lewis Chose Freedom Over Status

Lewis had always been driven. Promotions. Performance bonuses. Recognition.

But behind the title was a man drowning in stress. Sleepless nights. Constant travel. No time for his partner or his health.

Quietly, over the years, he'd been saving 30% of his income. He lived below his means, avoided lifestyle inflation, and invested consistently.

At 38, he realised: "I don't need more. I need different."

With two years of living expenses saved and passive income covering some essentials, he handed in his notice.

He now works three days a week doing purpose-driven work, cycles every morning, and volunteers at a local food bank.

He earns less, but feels infinitely wealthier.

> "I don't need to prove anything anymore," he says.
> "Wealth bought me that peace."

Your Wealth-Building Action for This Chapter

Redefine What Wealth Means to You

- Write your personal definition of wealth

- Focus on feelings, freedom, and choices, not just numbers

Link Each Financial Goal to a Life Freedom

For every savings or investment goal, answer:
"What will this allow me to do, feel, or avoid?"

Audit the "More" Trap in Your Life

Where are you chasing more without clarity?

What's "enough" for you in that area?

Create a Freedom Vision Board (Digital or Paper)

Instead of pictures of stuff, fill it with:

Places you want to go

Moments you want to experience

Emotions you want to feel

Look at it weekly to refocus your goals

✓ *Bonus Tip:* Take a "time audit" this week. Write down how you spend each hour of your day. Ask: "Is this how I want to live?" Let your answers guide your next money move.

Takeaway: Wealth Isn't the Destination, It's the Doorway

You don't build wealth just to have it.
You build wealth to use it, wisely.

To buy back your time.
To create peace of mind.
To live with intention, not obligation.

So don't get lost in the pursuit of more.
Focus instead on the pursuit of meaning.

Because the richest life isn't the one with the most stuff.
It's the one where **you get to choose**.

Chapter 20: Becoming a Wealth Builder for Life

When people think of wealth, they often imagine a finish line.

A magic number. A certain lifestyle. A sense of "I've made it."

But here's what the real wealth builders eventually learn:

> There is no finish line.
> There is only the next level of freedom, growth, and purpose.

Wealth isn't a one-time destination. It's a lifelong **practice**, a way of living, thinking, and choosing.

And the good news?

You don't need a six-figure salary, fancy degree, or perfect timing to live that way.

You just need a long-term mindset, and the courage to stay in the game.

Why Wealth-Building Is a Practice, Not a Goal

Too many people treat wealth like a sprint:

> "Once I hit £10,000 in savings, I'll relax."

> "Once I pay off debt, I'm done."

> "Once I get that raise, I'll finally feel secure."

But these are just **milestones**, not the full journey.

Wealth-building is more like brushing your teeth:

> You don't do it once and tick it off forever.

> You do it daily, because it maintains health and prevents problems.

It's the same with your money:

> Tracking your spending.

> Contributing to your investments.

> Making conscious choices.

> Learning, adjusting, and growing.

The real power isn't in how fast you reach a goal.
It's in how you **keep showing up**, year after year, habit after habit.

Staying Curious, Flexible, and Adaptive

The economy will change.
Jobs will change.
Your life will change.

So the question isn't: *"How can I set my finances and forget them?"*
It's: *"How can I stay curious, flexible, and ready to evolve?"*

💡 **Tips to Keep Growing:**

- **Read one money book a year** – keep your mindset fresh

- **Follow trusted financial voices** – filter out the noise

- **Review your goals quarterly** – realign with what matters

- **Be willing to pivot** – if your values shift, so should your financial strategy

Wealth isn't just about accumulation. It's about **adaptation**, so that your money serves you at every stage of life.

You Don't Need a Big Income, You Need Big Commitment

Let's say that again, because it's the heartbeat of this book:

> **You don't need a big income. You need big commitment.**

This entire journey is proof:

- People with £25,000 salaries paying off £15,000 in debt
- Minimum-wage workers building emergency funds
- Teachers becoming investors
- Admin assistants becoming landlords
- Quiet families building £100,000 net worths in ten years, without ever earning six figures

Their secret wasn't a big windfall.

It was:

A budget

A goal

A system

A refusal to give up

That's what wealth looks like.

Not flashy. But powerful.

Every Pound Matters: Save It. Invest It. Protect It.

You know what separates dreamers from wealth-builders?

They respect the value of **every single pound**.

£10 saved is a future bill paid

£50 invested is a seed for compound growth

£5 not spent on impulse is £5 that stayed in your pocket, and created discipline

Because wealth is not built on giant leaps.
It's built on **small, repeated decisions**.

Every pound is a vote for your future.
Every pound is a brick in your foundation.
Every pound is an act of self-respect.

Real Story: Yasmin, the Quiet Millionaire

Yasmin was never loud about money.

She worked as a school administrator. Lived in a modest semi-detached house. Drove a used car. Packed her lunch.

No one ever guessed she was building wealth.

But she was.

For over two decades, she:

- Saved 20–30% of her income

- Maxed out her pension contributions

- Bought a rental flat with savings from a side tutoring gig

- Lived below her means

Focused on needs, not status

At 54, her net worth quietly crossed the £1 million mark.

She didn't post it on Instagram. She didn't upgrade her life overnight.

She simply took a deep breath and smiled.

> "I built this quietly," she said.
> "And now I get to live loudly, in peace, freedom, and choice."

Your Wealth-Building Action for Life

You've made it to the final chapter, but this isn't the end.

It's the **beginning** of your lifelong journey as a wealth builder.

Here's how to keep that momentum alive:

1. Create a Personal Wealth Builder Manifesto

Write down your truths:

> "Wealth is a habit, not a number."

"Every pound I save or invest brings me closer to freedom."

"I am not my income, I am my choices."

Stick it on your fridge. Read it weekly.

2. Design a Simple Weekly Wealth Practice

Choose 3 habits to check in on:

- Did I track my spending?
- Did I contribute to savings/investments?
- Did I learn something new about money?

Make it a 15-minute Sunday ritual.

3. Mentor Someone Else

One of the best ways to stay accountable? **Teach someone else** what you've learned:

- A friend
- A family member
- A child

A colleague

You don't have to be perfect. Just honest. Share the journey. That keeps you growing, too.

Takeaway: You Are a Wealth Builder Now

If you've read this far, you've already proven one thing:

You care.

You're committed.

And you're capable of building wealth, on any income.

So let this be your declaration:

> "I am no longer waiting for more money to feel secure.
> I'm building wealth today, with what I have, where I am, who I am."
>
> "Because I don't need to earn big to live big.
> I just need to **act small, consistently, and intentionally**, for life."

Conclusion: You Already Have Enough to Start

If you've made it to this point, something inside you is shifting.

Maybe it's a spark of belief, finally seeing that wealth isn't some exclusive club for high earners and finance bros.

Maybe it's a quiet resolve, deciding you're done feeling stuck, done waiting for the perfect salary, the perfect time, or the perfect conditions.

Maybe, just maybe, you've started to see the truth:

You already have enough to start.

You don't need to make six figures.

You don't need a windfall, a wealthy family, or a finance degree.

You don't even need to get it all right from day one.

You just need to take the next small, brave step.

And then the one after that.

Because wealth is built *from the inside out*, with mindset, decisions, and habits, not with income brackets.

Don't Wait for More, Use What You've Got

Throughout this book, we've met people who:

- Paid off tens of thousands in debt on modest wages

- Saved emergency funds while earning minimum wage

- Invested small amounts consistently and built six-figure net worths

- Left stressful jobs, not because they struck it rich, but because they planned wisely

- Built lasting financial peace without ever looking "rich" on the outside

Their secret?

They stopped waiting.

They started using what they had:

£20 here

£50 there

An extra hour to budget

A mindset shift from "I can't" to "How can I?"

They didn't wait to be rich.
They *acted* like wealth builders.

And because of that, they *became* wealth builders.

Take One Small Wealth-Building Step Today

Before you close this book, make a commitment to yourself.

Not a grand, sweeping overhaul.

Just one step.

Open a free budgeting app

Cancel a subscription you no longer use

Put £10 into a savings pot and name it "Freedom Fund"

Automate a £20 monthly investment

Watch one video about index funds

Write down what wealth means to you

Whatever it is, do it today.

Because the first step is the only one you truly control. The rest? They'll follow if you just keep walking.

You Are Not Behind. You Are Beginning.

Maybe you've made money mistakes.

Maybe you've felt ashamed, stuck, or overwhelmed.

Maybe you've looked at your bank account and thought, "What's the point?"

Let me tell you: there *is* a point.

Because this is the moment you draw a line in the sand.

This is the moment you stop waiting for the perfect income or the perfect time.

This is the moment you build wealth, not with hype or pressure, but with grounded confidence.

You're not behind.
You're beginning.

And beginnings are powerful.

Final Words: You Don't Have to Earn More, You Just Have to Act Differently

Let's end where we began, with the truth most people never hear:

> **Wealth isn't how much you earn. It's what you do with what you earn.**

So go out there and *do* something with it.

Start small. Start imperfect. Start now.

Because you, right now, reading this sentence, you are already wealthy.

Not because of what you have.

But because of what you're about to do.

Thank you for reading. Now go build wealth, your way, starting today.

Alex Carter

Thank You for Reading.

If this book offered you clarity, calm, or a shift in how you see the world, I'd be truly grateful if you took a moment to share your thoughts in a **short Amazon review**.

Your reflection helps other readers discover timeless ideas that still matter today and keeps the philosophy alive for those who seek it.

Your words keep wisdom moving forward.

THE WEALTH SERIES

Alex Carter is an internationally recognised wealth mindset coach, financial empowerment speaker, and New York Times bestselling author. With over 20 years of experience in personal finance, entrepreneurship, and personal development, Alex has helped thousands transform their financial futures, not by chasing money, but by mastering their mindset.

Website: **edenrootpress.com**
Instagram: **edenroot.press**

How to Be Wealthy Mindset

7 Steps to Think Like a Millionaire

10 Secrets of Financially Successful People

How to Overcome a Scarcity Mindset and Embrace Abundance

How to Attract Money into Your Life

How to Stop Living Paycheck to Paycheck

7 Steps to Achieve Financial Freedom

How to Invest in Yourself for Big Returns

How to Earn What You're Worth

How to Overcome Fear of Success and Prosper

How to Stop Self-Sabotaging Your Finances

How to Make Money Work for You

How to Build Wealth on Any Income

5 Secrets to Thinking Big and Building Wealth

Printed in Dunstable, United Kingdom